WORK-APPLIED LEARNING
for Change

SELVA ABRAHAM

WAL PUBLICATIONS

Enquiries concerning these terms should be addressed to WAL Publications.

WAL Publications Pty Ltd
Level 1
27 Currie Street
Adelaide SA 5000
Australia

National Library of Australia Cataloguing-in-Publication entry:

Author:	Abraham, Selva, 1945-
Title:	Work-Applied Learning for Change / Selva Abraham.
ISBN:	9780987372109 (pbk.)
Subjects:	Organizational learning--Australia.
	Organizational change--Management.
	Executives--Training of--Australia.
	Chief executive officers--Training of--Australia.
Dewey Number:	658.4060994
ISBN:	978-0-9873721-0-9

Design and formatting by Barbara Velasco (Papel Papel)
Printed and bound by Lightning Source

CONTENTS

FOREWORD

"Leadership and learning are indispensable to each other."
- American President John F. Kennedy

Leadership and learning remain indispensible for the continued growth and prosperity of South Australian managers and their organisations.

Learning does not stop when we leave school; it is a lifelong journey and our workplaces provide us with new experiences and opportunities.

As a young law student, I could never have imagined the education, skills and experiences which awaited me in my role as a Senator for South Australia and previously as the former head of the union representing thousands of fast food and retail workers.

I commend the Australian Institute of Business for its strong belief in work-applied learning and research, enabling students to confidently bring their workplace experience into the classroom.

Practical experience meshes with academic pursuits and the students acquire invaluable insight into the challenges and potential opportunities back in the real world of business and management.

I welcome the publication of this book which offers fascinating examples of work-applied learning. Whether you work in the government, industry, health care or education sector, there is much to learn from its contents.

Senator the Hon. Don Farrell
Federal Parliament, Canberra

FOREWORD

Many have considered and debated the case for and against the interrelatedness of Action Learning and Action Research. Much debate has also occurred on the definitions and descriptions of Action Learning and Action Research. The consequence of such thought and opinion is a rich variety within the fields that are these meta-methodologies. Action Learning, Action Research Association Inc (ALARA) has long encouraged the debate and promotion of Action Learning and Action Research around the world.

For this reason, I welcome this book. As Selva Abrahams acknowledges (p. 6), there are many views on the meaning and method of implementation of Action Learning and Action Research. The Work-Applied Learning (WAL) model is an interesting example of going beyond the discussion of these variations and using a fused model to extract the most from the intervention for the client organisation. The "wheels within the wheels" of the mini-cycles within major cycles produces a highly flexible approach that creates learning for individuals, organisational learning, and rigour in the intervention.

The three examples from client organisations demonstrate these qualities in WAL. The reader will see the flexibility of WAL in the Global Carriers Group's example (Chapter 3). The organisation used the first major cycle of WAL for individual and organisational learning. The second major cycle helped the organisation deal with the Asian financial crisis of the late 1990s. The diverse project outcomes identified by the Papua New Guinea Internal Revenue Commission (p. 130) reflect the breadth of the impacts the methodology can have on an organisation. Outcomes included developing a business plan, creating understanding amongst the executive on their own roles and work practices, building stronger relationships and breaking down hierarchical barriers.

Selva Abraham and I have discussed the difficulty of gaining organisational commitment to Action Learning and Action Research. Organisations too often see the former as a fad and the latter as too theoretical or not rigorous enough. As described in this book, organisations can gain much from WAL, and the flexibility in methodology does not come at a compromise to measurable outcomes. As any good Action Learning / Action Research intervention requires, WAL is an evolving concept. Further enhancements and opinions are likely, and, I dare say, welcomed by Selva and AIB. ALARA, of course, will also welcome further debate and use of these methods.

Colin Bradley
President
Action Learning, Action Research Association Inc
www.alara.net.au

ABOUT THE AUTHOR

Selva Abraham MBA, PhD

Selva is the Chairman of the Australian Institute of Business (AIB), which he established as a management consultancy in 1984.

AIB has since evolved into a business school which offers undergraduate and postgraduate qualifications in business and management and which are accredited within the Australian Qualifications Framework. In fact, AIB is the first (and still the only) private business school in Australia that is authorised to offer doctoral programmes. In addition to its education programs, AIB also has a work-applied learning research centre and a consultancy arm, all oriented towards using action research, action learning, reflective practice and case research.

Selva obtained his MBA from Henley Management College – Brunel University, UK, and then his PhD from Flinders University, South Australia.

Over the years, Selva has been involved in many management development and change projects, working with private, public and community organisations. These include Motorola, Intel, Banque Nationale de Paris, Société Generale, Eastern Pretech, Australia Post, Light Regional Council, Aboriginal Sobriety Group to name but a few.

In addition to on-going consultancy projects, he has two action research books to his name and his current work at AIB includes leading a team of researchers in work-applied learning, using action research, action learning and reflective practice.

ABOUT THE CONTRIBUTORS

Colin Brimson MBA
Colin has worked for Australia Post for more than 40 years, and has served in several managerial roles for the past 25 years. He was State Manager, Delivery South Australia/Northern Territory for more than 10 years before being promoted to his current position of General Manager, MAIL Services South Australia/Northern Territory.

Mohamad Bin Hashim MBA, DBA
After serving in various managerial capacities at Shell Malaysia for 16 years, Mohamad started and grew a small domestic tanker business to an international shipping conglomerate, Global Carriers Berhad, which was listed on the Kuala Lumpur Stock Exchange in 1996. From 2003, he has pursued other business interests and is now Chairman of a major residential and commercial development company in Malaysia.

Alois Daton MBA, DBA
Alois has been with the Internal Revenue Commission, Papua New Guinea (IRC) for over 30 years. Since 2007, he has been the Commissioner of Tax at IRC. Prior to this appointment, he held different managerial positions in the Customs division, as well as in the Corporate Services and Tax Technical areas of IRC.

Dennis Hardy MA, PhD
Dennis has had a distinguished academic career at Middlesex University, UK, where he has held various senior management roles, including that of Deputy Vice-Chancellor. He specialises in the areas of local government strategy and urban planning and has a keen interest in work-applied learning and research. Currently, he is the Dean, Australian Institute of Business.

ACKNOWLEDGEMENTS

No matter how much one is fired to write a book, every author will know that one is also reliant on the contribution of others. This case is certainly no exception and I am grateful to a number of good friends and colleagues.

For a start, the book could not have been completed without the willingness of past and present research degree candidates and corporate clients of the Australian Institute of Business to share their findings. As the following pages will show, I am grateful, especially, to Colin Brimson, Mohamad Bin Hashim and Alois Daton for contributing chapters based on their own research and practice, and to Brian Carr for confirming the value of Work-Applied Learning in developing a group of senior managers in his own organisation. I am also indebted to Dennis Hardy, Dean of the Australian Institute of Business, for his invaluable feedback and encouragement in my journey of writing this book.

When it came to the production side of the project, I should like to thank Nathan Robert for preparing the diagrams, and Nicola Markus for making timely use of her proof-reading skills. Barbara Velasco executed the design to her usual high standards.

My two sons, Sanjay and Vinod, have helped me in ways that they would probably not themselves recognise. Their boundless energy and determination to make a success of the Australian Institute of Business has been a constant source of inspiration. In practical terms, by taking on more of the managerial and commercial duties that not so long ago I was performing myself, they have given me the space to engage in consulting, research and writing this book.

Most of all, my gratitude is directed to my wife and long-time business partner, Param. The precision derived from her legal background has, time and again, kept me on the right track. Her questioning, cajoling and, most of all, encouragement has given me the strength to pursue this challenging project to completion. She has been tireless in working with me at every stage.

In spite of this expert help on a variety of fronts, if there are any remaining errors and omissions, the responsibility for these rests with me.

PREFACE

It is now more than fifteen years since the publication of my earlier books on Action Research.[1] Since then there have been many developments to take into account.

Over time, I have been able to reflect on my original ideas and have found ways to take these forward. I have worked closely with subsequent cohorts of research candidates and with corporate clients; together, we have applied the Work-Applied Learning approach to solve a variety of 'real world' problems. Inevitably, in this ensuing period I have also enjoyed the advantage of reading what other writers have published, and I gratefully acknowledge the stimulus that this has provided. And, of course, even in this relatively short period the world itself has changed in so many ways, calling for a fresh appraisal of issues faced by today's managers.

For these various reasons, it was timely for me to return to the drawing board and produce something new. I am convinced that a Work-Based Learning approach, with Action Research and Action Learning (ARAL), remains every bit as valuable for managers as it was when I first ventured into the field. I am also convinced that, having tested it more widely in practice, it is even more robust than it was previously. It is this 'Mark 2' model that I am presenting in this book.

True to the spirit of Work-Applied Learning and ARAL, the book is a blend of concepts and practice. As well as my own ideas on the conceptual basis of this approach, I have been able to call on the experience of fellow researchers at the Australian Institute of Business. Thus, the book contains diverse examples to demonstrate the application of Work-Applied Learning and ARAL, as well as a further exploration of ideas. Nothing stands still, of course, and in the conclusion I point to an undiminished need to further refine the model as we continue to learn more. There is no end to the process, only further cycles of planning, acting, observing, reflecting and evaluating.

---

[1]Selva Abraham (1994) *Board Management Training for Indigenous Community Leaders Using Action Research: The Kuju CDEP Learning Experience.* South Australia: Port Lincoln Kuju CDEP Inc.; Selva Abraham (1997) *Exploratory Action Research for Manager Development.* Toowong, Queensland: ALARPM Inc.

CHAPTER 1

WORK-APPLIED LEARNING
AN ACTION RESEARCH AND ACTION LEARNING
(ARAL) PERSPECTIVE

INTRODUCTION

This chapter provides the background to the concept and practice of Work-Applied Learning (WAL) for change. I have been researching and testing this concept over the past thirty years, with practitioners and researchers as a management consultant and as a professor at the Australian Institute of Business (AIB) in Adelaide, South Australia. My initial readings and experiences in Work-Based Learning (WBL) led me to extend it to WAL through the use of a fused Action Research and Action Learning approach.

THE JOURNEY FROM WBL TO WAL

My experience in WBL started during a management training program for bankers in Singapore. I was part of a team of three consultants in the program, but as I was new in the consultancy, I was asked to observe and record the proceedings and make a contribution on practice if and when called upon. The other two consultants in the team were specialists in systems management and they presented their sessions by reading from a text by Louis Allen (1964) and explaining the theory. This they did for eight three-hour sessions held every other evening.

The only exciting aspect for me and the participants was that the two consultants took turns in presenting alternate sessions, but other than that, it was the same process of reading the text and explaining the theory. Some participants confided to me that they could do the reading themselves. I was bored, the participants were bored, and what shocked me the most was that at the end of the eight three-hour sessions, the two consultants believed they had done a wonderful job. I, on the other hand, believed that the program could have been delivered in a much more interesting manner. Because of this experience, I decided to look for opportunities that would help me to learn and grow my consultancy and presentation skills.

From 1971 to 1975, I gained invaluable experience in project management and general management in several organisations specialising in event management, marketing and public relations. During that time, I was one of the ten founders of the Marketing Institute of Singapore. The inaugural speaker for the Institute was Patrick Kehoe, who was then a university professor in Canada working closely with Bill Reddin (1970) on managerial effectiveness.

Patrick Kehoe and I subsequently explored the viability of working together and as a result, in 1975 we established a management development consultancy in Singapore. I managed this organisation as its executive director, working also as a management consultant, until 1983. It was a very enriching and meaningful experience under the mentorship of Patrick Kehoe as he coached me on how to facilitate management workshops.

The next step was to gain a postgraduate qualification through an MBA program. But the challenge was to find a program that would allow me to combine work and study. In 1979, I enrolled in the MBA program at Henley Management College in the UK as it suited my requirements. It was very fortunate that this program had a focus on WBL as I was able to resolve problems in my consultancy business by applying many of the concepts I had learnt. I completed the MBA in 1981 and during the following years secured several projects which enabled me to improve my management consultancy skills.

Since 1981, I have been exploring the use of the WBL process with private companies, banks, public sector entities and community organisations in Singapore, Malaysia and Australia. In 1984, I migrated to Australia, where I established a management development consultancy called Gibaran Management Consultants (Gibaran), now renamed as the Australian Institute of Business, which focused on WBL.

The results of my forays into exploring WBL were very encouraging. However, in the late 1980s, many participants on my programs started expressing an interest in obtaining a certificate to attest to their learning.

As a result, I entered into negotiations with the Australian Institute of Management (AIM) in South Australia to explore the viability of AIM providing certificates to managers who completed the programs delivered by my consultancy. After reviewing the content, assessment and quality of the work-applied Gibaran Management Development Program, AIM agreed to confer its Diploma of Management to all managers who successfully completed that program.

My desire to investigate further into WBL in the context of change management led me to undertake a PhD with Flinders University, South Australia where I investigated WAL using Action Research. I completed my PhD in 1993.

In 1994, the Mount Eliza Business School became the first private business school in Australia to be accredited to offer an MBA degree under the Australian Qualifications Framework. By then I had developed a senior management program, namely, the Gibaran Executive Development Program (GEDP). I presented to the then Chief Executive of the school, Dr Barry Ritchie, a proposal for the GEDP to be granted recognition as being equivalent to a postgraduate certificate.

After intensive scrutiny of the program by Dr Ritchie and his team, the GEDP was granted credit for the equivalent of one third of the Mount Eliza MBA program, which meant that participants who completed the GEDP were to be awarded the Mount Eliza Graduate Certificate in Management. There were two cohorts of the GEDP that benefited from this arrangement with Mount Eliza, but this ended in 1995 when its MBA program was merged with that of Monash University.

This incident made me determined to seek direct accreditation for Gibaran programs. As a result, over the next few years, Gibaran succeeded in obtaining accreditation within the Australian Qualifications Framework for the Bachelor of Business Administration, Master of Business Administration, Master of Management (Research, Master of Management (Work-Based Learning), Doctor of Business Administration and Doctor of Philosophy courses.

These courses used the work-applied research methods of action research, case research and reflective practice in varying degrees. Some of the academics who made major contributions to crafting the curricula and the rationale for these courses were Emeritus Professor Chad Perry, Professor Ron Passfield and Professor Peter OBrien.

Over the years, I have been reflecting on the views of various writers on WBL, including workplace learning (see footnote for writers)[1]. As a result, I have collated the main features of WBL and provide them in Table 1.1.

---

[1]Alderman and Milne (2005); Argyris (1994); the Australian National Training Authority ANTA (1998); Bassi, Cheney and Lewis (1998); Boud and Symes (2000); Costley (2001); Fox and Grey (2000); Garnett, Costley and Workman (2009); Helyer (2010), Jarvis, P., Holford, J. & Griffin, C. (2003)); Matthews (1999); Roodhouse and Mumford (2010); Nichols, (2000); Raelin (2000; 2008); Resnick (1987); Ruona, Lynham and Chemack (2003); Scribner (1986); Schon (1983); Watkins and Marsick (1992); Wenger, (1999; 2003).

Table 1.1 – Features of Work-Based Learning

Work-Based Learning:
- focuses on tasks
- is a collaborative activity resultant of an experience or problem for which there is a known knowledge base
- is different from what normally happens in business schools
- is a practical and cognitive process
- is learnt by working, not through reading or observing work
- has a variety of instructional strategies away from the classroom
- is self-directed; creative; expressive; involves feeling; is continual and reflective
- includes action projects, learning teams and other inter-personal experiences, including mentorship
- provides opportunities for professional practice, critical analysis and reflective thinking
- involves knowledge creation and utilisation as collective activities when learning becomes everyone's job.
- involves thinking, and evaluating theory and practice
- links coursework assessment with workplace practices
- can lead to the attainment of qualifications

It can be seen from the above table that WBL appears to focus on learning in the workplace by individuals or as teams, for the purpose of application. However, while facilitating and researching various WBL programs over the years, I have developed and refined a model which is an extension of WBL. I have termed it the Work-Applied Learning (WAL) model. In addition to creating learning in the workplace by individuals or as teams, the use of this WAL model has also resulted in the collective learning of the teams to create organisational learning and change. The WAL model is described in the next section.

WORK-APPLIED LEARNING MODEL

The WAL model that I have developed recognises the workplace as the crucible of learning for change. This model has been specifically researched in the context of Work-Applied Learning for managers to learn and introduce change. While incorporating the features of WBL, WAL is grounded in a fused Action Research method and Action Learning process ("ARAL"). It is the addition of the ARAL approach which leads to not only individual learning by the managers and team learning, but also organisational learning and change as the managers and their teams plan, act, observe, reflect, evaluate and validate work-based projects through the action research (AR) cycles of WAL. Figure 1.1 illustrates the learning and change through AR cycles.

Figure 1.1 – Learning and Change through AR cycles.

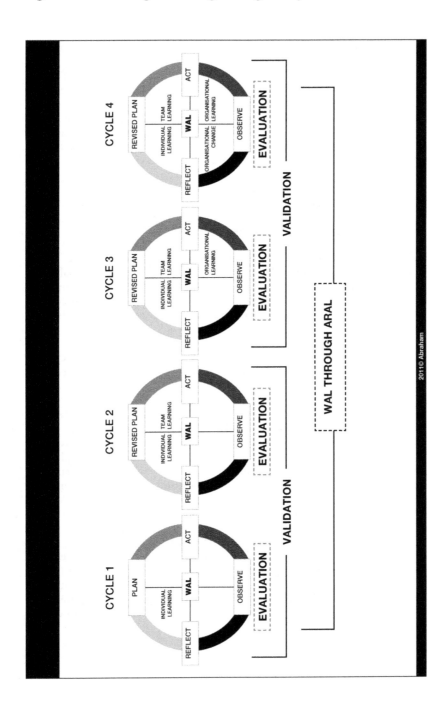

The following section will describe the ARAL approach.

FUSING ACTION RESEARCH AND ACTION LEARNING (ARAL)

Action Research is a practical research method and should not be confused with the Action Learning process.

Lewin's (1946, 1947, 1951, 1952) concept of Action Research and Revans' (1982) concept of Action Learning are similar in some respects as both are problem-focused, action-oriented and utilise group dynamics; however, they differ in a number of major respects. Revans (1983) is more interested in encouraging "questioning insight" than in solving problems. In his own words, Revans (1983, p.11) said:

> Action Learning... requires questions to be posed in conditions of ignorance, risk and confusion, when nobody knows what to do next; it is only marginally interested in finding the answers once those questions have been posed.

Action Research, on the other hand, was designed as a means by which change could be introduced in problematic situations to bring about a noticeable improvement. Revans places more emphasis on the development of managers' skills and abilities than Lewin, who was more concerned with making a contribution to science, and he accords outside experts a far lesser role.

Lastly, while Revans admits that Action Learning can become a cyclical process, it is not essentially cyclical in nature like Lewin's concept of Action Research.

There is another aspect, however, in which Action Research and Action Learning are alike. The original concepts first voiced by Revans and Lewin have not stood the test of time intact and inviolate. Rather, opinions about what Action Learning and Action Research mean and how to implement them are many and varied. Consequently, every group that wants to undertake an Action Learning project or an Action Research program must consider these various opinions and then decide what form of research or learning is appropriate for its needs.

In my study of Work-Applied Management Development using Action Research (Abraham 1997), I identified twelve Action Research characteristics that emerged in my research. Peters and Robinson (1984) in their survey of the literature on Action Research characteristics also noted most of the same characteristics. Table 1.2 provides a summary of the twelve characteristics of Action Research which I have refined over my years of research.

Table 1.2 – General Characteristics of Action Research

	CHARACTERISTIC	SUMMARY DESCRIPTION
1	Problem Focus	The Action Research method is problem-focussed in the context of real life situations. The solving of such problems in a research sense would contribute to professional practice and the development of social science knowledge.
2	Action Orientation	The diagnosis of a problem and the development of a plan to solve the problem can only be considered to be action-oriented if the action becomes part of a process to implement the plan. This brings an action element to the solving of an immediate problem of the organisation which has strategic change implications for the said organisation.
3	Cyclical Process	The Action Research method involves cycles of planning, action, observation, and reflection (evaluation). Thus, the cycles of the Action Research method allow the group members to develop a plan, to act, to observe and to reflect on this plan, to implement the plan and then to modify the plan, based on the needs of the group members and the requirements of the organisation and situation. A record of the processes of each cycle enables its strengths and weaknesses to be reviewed so that modifications and strategies can be developed for future cycles.
4	Collaboration	Collaboration is a fundamental ingredient of the Action Research method, because without a team effort to solve problems in an environment of participation, Action Research cannot exist. Collaboration on group problems using the Action Research method can be viewed as a continuum from total dependence on the facilitator, who acts as a leader directing the group problem-solving process, through to the total management of the problem by the group members with the facilitator acting as a resource person. The position of the facilitator and the group on this continuum depends on the situation and the needs of the group.

Table 1.2 – General Characteristics of Action Research (contd.)

	CHARACTERISTIC	SUMMARY DESCRIPTION
5	Ethical Practice	Community interests, improvements in the lives of the group members, justice, rationality, democracy and equality are some of the themes of 'ethical' behaviour. The ethical basis of Action Research is an important characteristic to consider, because the Action Research method involves, to a large extent, groups of people with limited power who are open to exploitation. It requires the researcher to concede their personal needs so that the needs of the group are given the highest priority.
6	Group Facilitation	The success of the Action Research method will depend on how well the group can operate as an effective team. An understanding of group dynamics therefore seems essential in facilitating this process and dealing with problems that arise during the Action Research cycles
7	Creative Thinking	The AR Group members will experience creative thinking as they go through stages of saturation, deliberation, incubation, and illumination where the group members look for different options and seek the opinions of different relevant parties to validate those options.
8	Learning and Re-education	Action Research can be viewed as re-educative, since it contributes to a change in the knowledge base of the organisation, a change in the skills, attitudes and knowledge of the individual group members, and a change in the skills and knowledge of the researcher. It also makes a contribution to several of the social sciences.
9	Naturalistic	If one accepts that Action Research should be scientific but that there are problems in adopting a positivistic model of science and applying it to social science settings, then it follows that a naturalistic approach is appropriate for the Action Research method. The approach involves qualitative descriptions recorded as case studies rather than laws of cause and effect tested experimentally with statistical analysis of data.

Table 1.2 – General Characteristics of Action Research (contd.)

	CHARACTERISTIC	SUMMARY DESCRIPTION
10	Emancipatory	The changes experienced by the group members during the Action Research process can contribute to some improvements in their lives and may also have wider social action and reform.
11	Normative	The normative characteristic of Action Research implies that the social 'norms' of the group are not only considered during the research, but, in order to bring about change in the group, they are modified during the Action Research process.
12	Scientific	Since the Action Research method does have a scientific basis and can provide an alternative to the positivistic view of science, it is essential that the research be conducted in such a way that it can be defended against criticisms of lack of scientific rigour.

In the 1990s, Graham Arnold, Rod Oxenberry and I (Abraham, Arnold & Oxenberry 1996) wrote on the fusing of Action Research and Action Learning in the context of organisational learning and change, and developed a word formula to capture the integrated nature of Action Research and Action Learning (ARAL).

We (Abraham et al, 1996) first identified the features specified by some authors as being necessary "ingredients" to produce Action Research and Action Learning and expressed them in word formulae as follows, with the symbols used being explained in Table 1.3:

Action Learning:

$$S + P + A \; (+F) \rightarrow AL$$

Action Research:

$$G + P + A + F + C + R \rightarrow AR$$

A scrutiny of the above formulae reveals that the only differences are i) the Action Research method includes a facilitator, whereas it could be optional in the Action Learning process, depending on the situation; and ii) the Action Learning process requires an Action Learning set whereas the Action Research method requires an Action Research Group.

Table 1.3 – Symbols Used in the Word Formulae (Abraham et al, 1996, p.17)

SYMBOLS	DESCRIPTION
S	The Action Learning <u>set</u> comprising individuals who come together to investigate solutions to shared problems and to learn from each other. There is no requirement that the set members are from the same organisation.
P	The <u>problem</u> to be addressed. Both Action Learning and Action Research share this problem-focused characteristic.
A	Both Action Research and Action Learning are <u>action</u>-oriented. The group or set takes positive action in response to the ideas and suggestions generated through questioning and discussion.
G	The nature of the Action Research <u>group</u> may be rather different to the set described in Action Learning. The group comprises members of an organisation or community and could also include "Researchers" who may be seen as an integral part of the group since they work in a collaborative manner with the group for change and knowledge development.
F	The term "<u>Facilitator</u>" has been placed in brackets in the action learning word formula to indicate the disparate views amongst the authors on whether or not a facilitator should be part of the set.
C	The <u>cyclical</u> nature of Action Research. Lewin (1946 and 1947) indicated that the spiral nature of steps was fundamental to Action Research. His steps started with diagnosis, followed by cycles of planning, action and reflection.
R	The <u>Researcher</u> in Lewin's original view assisted the group. While some writers question the need for a Researcher, the role of a Researcher as a consultant to the group is widely supported by other authors.
AL	Action Learning
AR	Action Research

This suggests that, in fact, Action Learning could be considered as a subset of Action Research. As a result, Abraham, et al (1996) proposed the ARAL model that fuses Action Learning and Action Research as follows: **AL + C + R → AR.**

The following section describes a typical WAL program which incorporates the fused ARAL model and shows how managers and their teams experience creative learning as they go through a WAL program.

THE WAL PROGRAM IN ACTION

A typical WAL program comprises a number of AR cycles and the phases within each AR cycle are as follows:

- AR group meetings;
- Knowledge Workshops;
- Work-Based Phases;
- joint observations and reflections; and
- monitoring and evaluation of the cycle.

Figure 1.2 shows the cycles of WAL with summaries of the phases.

Where an AR cycle spreads out from six to nine months, it is possible to have several AR mini-cycles embedded within. Each AR mini-cycle would have the same phases as the AR cycles but compressed in a shorter timeframe.

All through the WAL program, four different types of facilitative roles emerge. These are the Facilitative Consultant; the Facilitative Tutor; the Facilitative Leader; and the Facilitative Trainer.

Descriptions of these facilitative roles are provided in the different phases of the WAL program in the following sections of this chapter.

AR GROUP MEETINGS

In a typical WAL program, the AR group normally includes a Facilitative Consultant, appointed by the client organisation, the managers involved in the program as participants, the chief executive and relevant stakeholders.

The Facilitative Consultant is either an internal or external change agent specialised in WAL with conceptual knowledge and practice in change management.

The Facilitative Consultant helps in the establishment of the AR group and works with the AR group in: the WAL program design; clarification of the organisational problem; identification of the organisational change project (change project); mentoring the individual managers in the change project and individual departmental team projects; and reflecting with and coaching the managers as they implement departmental projects with their team members.

Figure 1.2 – AR Cycles within the WAL Program

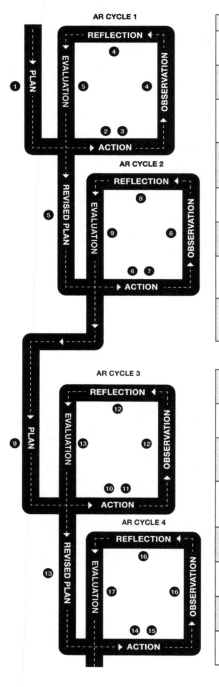

1. First AR Group meeting.

2. Knowledge Workshop: Facilitative Tutor's input on management knowledge. Reflection against Work-Based Project issues.

3. Work-Based Phase: Managers apply their knowledge during the Work-Based Phase with their action learning teams.

4. Joint observation and reflection by the Facilitative Consultant and managers on the Knowledge Workshop and Work-Based Phase.

5. Second AR Group meeting: First Monitoring and evaluation session with CEO, the managers and the Facilitative Consultant. Re-planning for Cycle 2.

6. Knowledge Workshop: Facilitative Tutor's input on management knowledge. Reflection against work-based issues.

7. Work-Based Phase. Managers apply their learning during the Work-Based Phase with their action learning teams.

8. Joint observation and reflection by the Facilitative Consultant and managers on the Knowledge Workshop and Work-Based Phase.

9. Third AR Group meeting: Second monitoring and evaluation session with CEO, the managers and the Facilitative Consultant. Re-planning for Cycle 3.

10. Knowledge Workshop: Facilitative Tutor's input on management knowledge. Reflection against work-based project issues.

11. Work-Based Phase. Managers apply their learning during the Work-Based Phase with their action learning teams.

12. Joint observation and reflection by the Facilitative Consultant and managers on the Knowledge Workshop and Work-Based Phase.

13. Fourth AR Group meeting. Third monitoring and evaluation session with CEO, the managers and the Facilitative Consultant. Re-planning for Cycle 4.

14. Knowledge Workshop: Facilitative Tutor's input on management knowledge. Reflection against work-based issues.

15. Work-Based Phase. Managers apply their learning during the Work-Based Phase with their action learning teams.

16. Joint observation and reflection by the Facilitative Consultant and managers on the knowledge workshop and Work-Based Phase.

17. Sixth AR Group meeting. Fourth monitoring and evaluation session with CEO, the managers and the Facilitative Consultant.

The Facilitative Consultant also provides conceptual knowledge during the knowledge workshops on ARAL and organisational change, facilitative leadership and reflective practice. These workshops are supplemented by reading materials, videos, and access to the online library. Web conferencing could also be used in place of these workshops.

The Facilitative Consultant continually guides the AR group members to critically review, reflect and evaluate the WAL program and the projects against the performance indicators of organisational change and departmental project outcomes; the ARAL process; individual and teamlearning.

At the first AR group meeting, the AR group will normally:

i)   clarify the organisational problem that is to be addressed, identify a change project to be undertaken by the managers and also establish departmental projects for each manager's team;

ii) agree on the WAL program design, including: the number and duration of workshop days; the number and duration of the Work-Based Phases; the number of mentoring and reflective sessions; the time allocated for each manager for feedback; and the scheduling of dates, taking into account the job demands and organisational culture;

iii) establish performance indicators for the change project; and

iv) clearly establish and agree upon the program objectives and the terms, conditions, obligations and commitments of the parties, namely the chief executive of the organisation, the managers, and the Facilitative Consultant.

Whilst the first AR group meeting would normally be face-to-face, subsequent meetings could be held on a face-to-face basis or as web-conference meetings. During these meetings, the managers would share their experiences from the Work-Based Phases and discuss the project outcomes, process outcomes and learning outcomes that are to be achieved and any deviations that they would like to be corrected.

KNOWLEDGE WORKSHOP PHASES

The Knowledge Workshops (either face to face or by web-conferencing) could range from one day to four days, depending on the needs of the managers and the demands of the organisation. The managers will be introduced to business and management concepts (for example: strategy; marketing; finance; human resources; operations; and leadership) including application relevant to the change project by a Facilitative Tutor who has relevant postgraduate qualifications and experience in that knowledge area. The Facilitative Tutor could be either an external person or an employee of the organisation.

This knowledge provided is supplemented by distance learning and reading materials and an online library. The Facilitative Tutors will show the managers the relevance of the knowledge to their change project. The managers are encouraged to question their change project, think critically about how to apply the knowledge to the project, how to scope and reflect on the project, and how to develop a draft plan for implementation using ARAL. This is the Work-Applied Learning experience that managers go through, not only during the Knowledge Workshops, but also when working with their teams during the Work-Based Phases.

Also during the Knowledge Workshops, the Facilitative Tutors will work closely with the managers to establish their departmental projects. Each departmental project would be established based on the needs of the department or division of the manager and would be linked to the change project. At the end of the first Knowledge Workshop, the managers would be required to present a draft plan for the change project, including the departmental projects that are integrated with the change project.

Table 1.4 provides a template for an ARAL change project plan. It can also be adapted for departmental project plans and be used by the managers to share their plans with their management.

Table 1.4 – ARAL Change Project Plan Template

The need for the project: • Describe the background to the issue or the problem that led to the project being chosen • Provide evidence to show that there is a need to resolve this problem or issue.
The purpose and outcomes of the project: • In a precise and concise manner, establish the purpose of the project. • What are the project outcomes that are to be achieved? • What is the expected learning outcome of the managers of the team and why? • What are the process outcomes?
The Learning Team: • Who are the members of the learning team? • Justify why they qualify as a member of the team. • What are the expected learning outcomes of each of these members? • What activities are to be put in place to achieve the project outcomes? • What type of budget is needed to achieve the project objective? • What is the timeframe and cost for the achievement of the project and learning outcomes.
The justification: • Justify why the change plan is action research- based. • Justify why the departmental projects are action learning projects.

WORK-BASED PHASES

Each Knowledge Workshop is followed by a Work-Based Phase, during which time the managers will return to their workplace. After the first Knowledge Workshop, they will be equipped with knowledge and process skills as facilitative leaders.

The managers as facilitative leaders guide their departmental team members (learning team) in their workplace to plan and implement the work-based projects.

As the managers go through the WAL program, they will become more knowledgeable about the concepts of facilitative leadership and Action Learning which they would have acquired through the Knowledge Workshops and which are supplemented by reading materials and access to an online library.

During the Work-Based Phase, the managers will work with their learning teams to:

- clarify the department's problem;
- identify the project;
- plan the departmental project to resolve the problem;
- refine the scope of their departmental projects;
- clearly establish the project outcomes;
- establish their own learning outcomes as well as the learning outcomes of the learning team members;
- establish the process outcomes;
- obtain the support of their management and, if necessary, further refine the departmental projects as agreed with management;
- implement the project as a departmental team using an Action Learning process.
- undertake directed reading on: the knowledge area required; facilitation leadership skills and group dynamics (this directed reading should continue all through the project implementation phases);
- establish working relationships between learning team members and other departments;
- ensure opportunities for effective reflection and review by their learning team members;
- keep detailed diary notes of the process as well as the project outcomes and learning outcomes;
- establish and continually encourage a working relationship between the learning team members; and
- consult and reflect with the chief executive and vital stakeholders as well as resource experts when required.

During the Work-Based Phase, there could arise a need for the learning team members to obtain competency based training to assist them in the implementation of the project. Such knowledge could be provided by a Facilitative Trainer.

The Facilitative Trainer would help the learning team members acquire competence in a relevant business or management area and understand how it is applied to their projects. This process is undertaken through workshops and directed reading. The Facilitative Trainer could be either an external person or an employee of the organization and must have a qualification in the relevant business or management area and also practical experience in that area.

At the end of these workshops, the learning team members will have the competency necessary to complete the projects. The managers and the Facilitative Trainer will work together to reflect and provide support to the learning team members.

As managers and their learning teams plan and implement their departmental projects, they undergo a Work-Applied Learning experience. The Work-Applied Learning experience can be summarised in a word formula as $K + P_1 + Q = P_2$. Figure 1.3 illustrates the Work-Applied Learning formula and the relationship between Work-Based Learning and Work-Applied Learning.

Figure 1.3 – The Work Applied Learning Formula

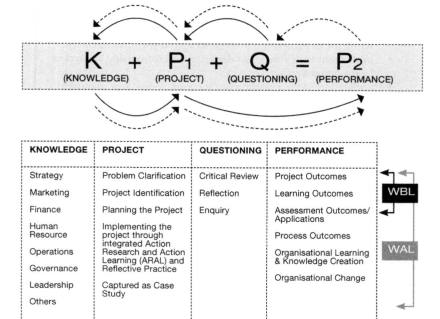

$$K + P_1 + Q = P_2$$

(KNOWLEDGE) (PROJECT) (QUESTIONING) (PERFORMANCE)

KNOWLEDGE	PROJECT	QUESTIONING	PERFORMANCE	
Strategy	Problem Clarification	Critical Review	Project Outcomes	
Marketing	Project Identification	Reflection	Learning Outcomes	WBL
Finance	Planning the Project	Enquiry	Assessment Outcomes/ Applications	
Human Resource	Implementing the project through integrated Action Research and Action Learning (ARAL) and Reflective Practice		Process Outcomes	
Operations			Organisational Learning & Knowledge Creation	WAL
Governance			Organisational Change	
Leadership	Captured as Case Study			
Others				

Whilst managers reflect on questions in the context of their projects, they experience creative thinking through stages of saturation, deliberation, incubation and illumination as they allow their minds to look for different options. They then seek opinions of other independent parties to validate those options.

The stages of the creative thinking process were initially formulated by Graham Wallace (1926) and since then they have been commented upon and adapted by different writers, including Tripathi and Reddy (2007). One such adaptation is provided below:

> **Saturation:** Becoming thoroughly familiar with a problem, with its setting, and more broadly, with activities and ideas akin to the problem.
>
> **Deliberation:** Mulling over these ideas, analysing them, challenging them, rearranging them, and thinking of them from several viewpoints.
>
> **Illumination:** A bright idea strikes, a bit crazy perhaps, but new and fresh and full of promise; you sense that it might be the answer.
>
> **Incubation:** Relaxing, turning off the conscious and purposeful search, forgetting the frustrations of unproductive labour, letting the subconscious mind work.
>
> **Accommodation:** Clarifying the idea, seeing whether it fits the requirements of the problem as it did on first thought, re-framing and adapting it, putting it on paper, getting other people's reaction to it.

During the continuous steps of creative thinking, managers learn as they move from a stage of unawareness to awareness, comprehension, conviction and finally, to actioning their work-based projects.

Whilst these five stages of communication and learning were originally used in the context of marketing communications and external customers, they are equally relevant to internal customers, namely managers and staff of organisations. Thus, Wimmer, R (2011) writes:

> All people pass through these stages for every decision they make or anything they learn.
>
> 1. All people pass through the stages at different speeds
>   – there is no universal timing.
> 2. Not all people make it to the Action stage.

The only way to move people through the five stages is through *repetition of message*. In most cases, people do not make decisions (or learn something) after only one exposure to a message. The process nearly always requires several exposures.

Figure 1.4 captures the cyclical creative thinking and learning process in WAL as the managers and their teams plan, act, observe, reflect, evaluate and validate their work-based projects through the AR cycles. At the core of this thinking and learning process is the WAL formula of K + P1 + Q = P2.

Figure 1.4 – The Cyclical Work-Applied Creative Learning Experience

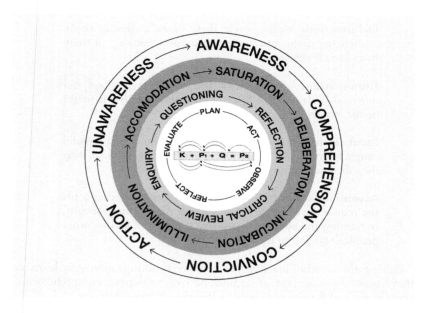

JOINT OBSERVATIONS AND REFLECTIONS

Typically at the end of each Work-Based Phase, the Facilitative Consultant will contact the managers either on a one-to-one basis or on a group basis, to seek their feedback on how the program is progressing and whether any further customisation is needed in the next cycle to make the program more effective.

EVALUATION OF THE CYCLES

After the joint observations and reflection session, the managers, the Facilitative Consultant and other AR Group members will come together for an evaluation meeting. The data collected by the Facilitative Consultant during the joint observations and reflections phase will be discussed and the opinions will be triangulated and evaluated and re-planning of the WAL program will be undertaken.

During this meeting, the AR Group members will analyse the performance outcomes and evaluate the project outcomes, the process outcomes and the learning outcomes of the managers and their learning teams. They will also evaluate whether the AR characteristics are observed and are prevalent throughout the WAL program.

VALIDATION

Typically, a WAL program is validated at the end of every two cycles. The validation is undertaken at a meeting of the AR Group as well as other stakeholders such as direct supervisors of the managers, the human resource director and members of the Board of Directors or other relevant persons.

The managers will present reports on their current progress and other issues in the WAL program against the performance indicators, seek feedback from those present and make necessary changes to the program and their performance.

The evaluation and validation phases of the various AR cycles are depicted in Figure 1.5.

CASE SUMMARIES OF TWO WAL PROGRAMS

This section provides case summaries of two WAL programs which show the link between the WAL model discussed previously and the actual planning and implementation of the WAL programs. The two case summaries are firstly, on the Light Regional Council (LRC) in South Australia and secondly, an international bank (which has not been named for reasons of privacy).

Case 1 – Planning the WAL Program for LRC

Program Background

The Light Regional Council (LRC) is a Local Government Area north of Adelaide, South Australia and includes the towns of Kapunda, Freeling and Roseworthy. LRC wanted to investigate ways in which they could embark upon a unique governance and community engagement process in planning and development matters. The LRC area had experienced substantial growth over the previous thirty years, and continuing expansion had resulted in an increase in staff.

Figure 1.5 – The Evaluation and Validation Process in WAL Programs

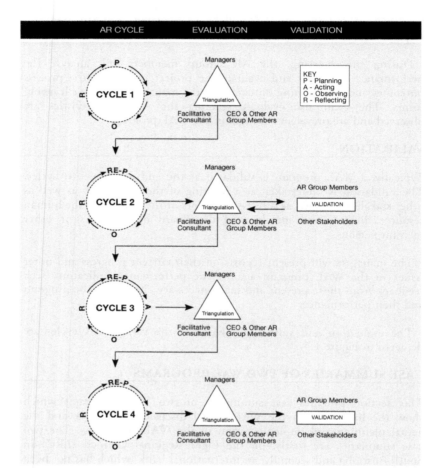

The LRC recognised that its managers would need further training and skills development if such governance and community engagement was to be successful. As a first step, they sought professional assistance from the Australian Institute of Business (AIB) to design an appropriate WAL program for six of their senior managers.

This program was titled the Work-Applied Strategic Management Development Program.

AR Group

As part of the WAL program, an Action Research (AR) Group was established. The AR Group was made up of the LRC Chief Executive Officer, Brian Carr, the six senior managers who would be the program participants, and a Facilitative Consultant of AIB.

In the first AR Group meeting, the CEO, the six managers and the Facilitative Consultant agreed on two major group projects and individual projects to be undertaken.

The two group projects identified were:

    i)   to review and update the current strategic plan of LRC; and
   ii) to develop a change management plan for LRC using ARAL.

The AR Group reviewed the proposed design of a typical mini-cycle in the WAL program provided by the Facilitative Consultant. Figure 1.6 shows the proposed design.

The AR Group members agreed on measurable outcomes for the program which are provided in Table 1.5.

Table 1.5 – Measurable Outcomes

On completing the WAL program, the managers would be able to:
- apply the knowledge gained to review the current strategic plan for the LRC and to update it for a period of four years;
- apply the concepts of change management, facilitative leadership and the ARAL process in designing a change management plan for their implementation; and
- work with the departmental teams in the planning and the implementation of the departmental sub-projects.

Figure 1.6 – A Typical Mini-cycle of a WAL Program

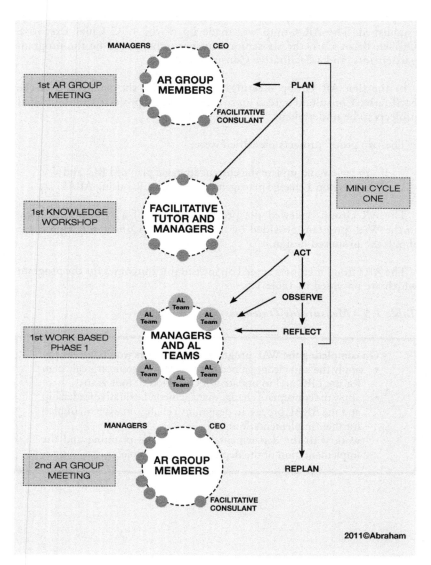

The AR group also established the obligations of all the relevant parties in the program and these are listed in Table 1.6.

Table 1.6 – Obligations of the Parties

LRC responsibilities:
- to identify the managers who would be participants in the WAL program;
- to establish an Action Research Group to work closely with the Facilitative Consultant in customising the program over the period of time, as well as to monitor, reflect and evaluate the program;
- to provide the managers with access to technical resources or research data, when required, and to rationalise and justify the strategic and change plans;
- to co-ordinate the Coaching and Reflective Sessions;
- to ensure that the instalments of the project reports are submitted to the Facilitative Consultant and CEO at least seven days before each Coaching and Reflective Session;
- to ensure the final group and individual project reports are submitted to the Facilitative Consultant, Facilitative Tutors and CEO for review and comments within six months of the commencement date of the program; and
- to pay fees and any related costs to AIB.

Obligations of the Facilitative Consultant and Facilitative Tutors:
- to participate in the customising of the WAL program with the AR group;
- to facilitate the workshops;
- to provide Coaching and Reflective Sessions to the managers at pre-arranged times;
- to review the instalments of the project reports produced by each manager, in order to give them feedback;
- to participate as a member of the AR Group in monitoring, reflecting and evaluating the progress of the program; and
- to provide feedback on the final group and individual project reports.

Managers' Obligations
- to undertake required readings during the program;
- to attend all the workshops;
- to work with their teams and with other managers, as required, to complete the group project reports and individual project reports and initiate implementation;
- to participate in the Coaching and Reflective Sessions with the Facilitative Consultant and FacilitativeTutors; and
- to finalise and submit the group project reports and individual project reports by the due date as agreed with the Facilitative Tutors.

At the end of the first AR Group meeting, the AR Group agreed that the review and update of the strategic plan would be completed within six months and that the strategic planning project would include the following individual projects: i)workforce planning; ii) infrastructure planning and maintenance planning; iii) long-range financial planning; iv) governance planning; and v) systems improvement planning.

The AR Group also agreed that they would focus on the second major group project, namely, the change management plan project, after the completion of the strategic planning project.

One of the six managers was the General Manager of Strategic Planning of the LRC. It was agreed that he would be the LRC representative for the strategic planning project and the other five managers would be responsible for the five individual projects.

Figure 1.7 illustrates the integration of the five individual projects with the strategic planning project.

Figure 1.7 – LRC Strategic Planning Project

The CEO encouraged the managers to work towards the Australian Institute of Business (AIB) Graduate Certificate in Management qualification, since this could be acquired if they completed academic assignments in addition to the group project reports and individual project reports.

THE WAL PROGRAM CYCLES

The WAL program would comprise one major AR cycle, with four AR mini- cycles, each of which had a AR Group meeting; a Knowledge Workshop; a Work-Based Phase; joint observations/reflections and evaluation. During the major AR cycle, there would be two validation sessions, one midway and the other at the end of the program.

The four mini-cycles within the major cycle are depicted in Figure 1.8. Four two-day Knowledge Workshops would be held at regular intervals over a period of six months. During the workshops, the managers would be introduced to the concepts, practice and process of strategy, change, facilitative leadership, WAL, Action Research, Action Learning and reflective practice.

The managers would be encouraged by the Facilitative Tutors to reflect critically on how to apply these concepts in an integrated manner as they:

i)   update the LRC's four-year strategic planning document; and
ii) reflect on their learning as Facilitative Leaders in their individual project reports.

In consultation with the Facilitative Consultant and Facilitative Tutors, the managers would identify various resource experts in financial planning, infrastructure and maintenance planning, systems improvement planning, governance planning and workforce planning to help them to undertake and finalise their individual project reports.

Each Knowledge Workshop would be followed by a Work-Based Phase of one month as shown in Figure 1.8. During each Work-Based Phase, the managers would return to their workplace and work with their Action Learning teams to develop their sub-project plans as their contribution to the strategic planning document.

The managers would also work together to develop the first major project (the review and update of the strategic plan) and during this process, consult and reflect with the Chief Executive Officer.

Throughout each Work-Based Phase, the six managers would reflect and record their facilitative leadership learning and experiences in the form of individual project reports.

A fortnight after each Knowledge Workshop, the managers would submit instalments of their individual project reports and the major project report for review by the Facilitative Tutors.

Figure 1.8 – LRC Knowledge Workshops and Work-Based Phases

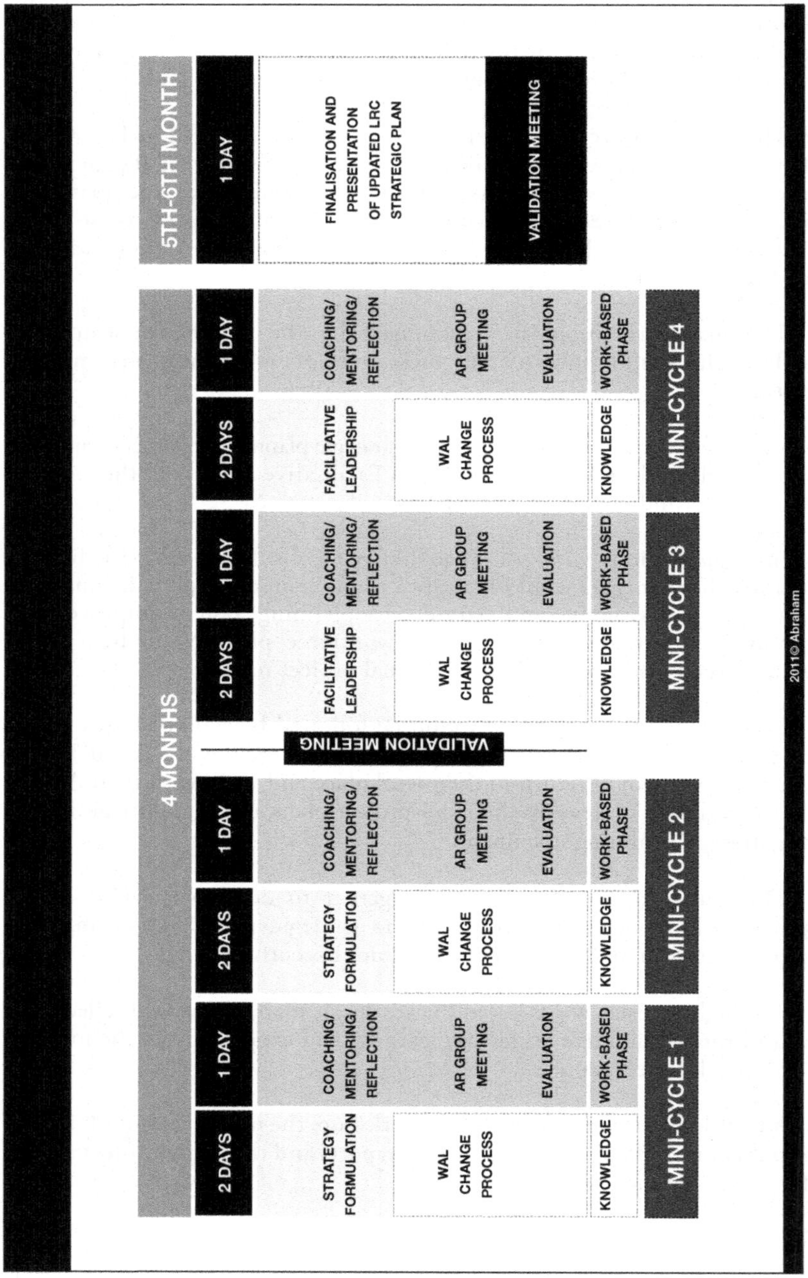

Three weeks after each Knowledge Workshop, the managers would have a Coaching and Reflection Session with the Facilitative Consultants on their major group project report on a group basis and their individual project reports on a one-to-one basis. At the end of the Work-Based Phase of each mini-cycle, an AR Group meeting would be held to reflect and evaluate the program based on the observations of the Facilitative Consultant, the Facilitative Tutors and the managers against the performance indicators of the program.

This program would be formally validated by a Steering Committee comprising the LRC Mayor, the Chief Executive Officer, Emeritus Professor Dennis Hardy and myself. This Steering Committee would meet twice, at the midway point of the program and again at the end of the program. During these two validation sessions, the managers would present to the Steering Committee the project outcomes, the process outcomes and the learning outcomes of the WAL program and reflect on their plans for implementing change.

Case 2 - WAL Program for an International Bank

Program Background

The management of an international bank was concerned that there was an increase in apathy towards its customers by the staff in many of its branches. This was confirmed by numerous letters of complaint from customers. One of the other concerns of management was that although frontline staff and bank officers were technically competent in banking, many lacked customer relations skills. The management believed that a Customer Relations Program needed to be planned and implemented for the bank officers and front-line staff of all its branches.

As a first step, the management decided that 60 bank officers and 200 front-line staff, chosen from across all the branches, should be exposed to the concepts and practice of effective customer relations. They suggested that the program for the officers and front-line staff be run separately and be integrated into their workplace.

This Work-Applied Customer Relations Program had two Action Research cycles, comprising AR Group meetings, Knowledge Workshops, observations and reflections, evaluation and validation.

Cycle 1

First AR Group Meeting

The AR Group for this program was made up of the Training Manager of the bank and two external Facilitative Consultants. The first AR Group meeting established the objectives of the program, the program design and the terms of the working relationship between the Facilitative Consultants and the Training Manager. It was decided that a select group of bank officers would be part of the AR Group as the program progressed.

The objectives of this program as agreed by the AR Group were to:

- provide the bank officers with an understanding of the concepts and practice of customer relations and how this could be used to develop a closer working relationship with their front-line staff and bank customers
- facilitate the bank officers to work in teams to develop a customer relations guide for the front-line staff
- coach and mentor the Training Manager to develop facilitation skills and undertake facilitation
- validate the customer relations guide with the front-line staff during their two-day workshops; and
- develop and launch a customer relations campaign to further emphasise the importance of customer relations in all the branches.

The design of the Customer Relations Program had three components:

- Customer Relations Training for the 60 bank officers – these bank officers were divided into five groups of twelve each, called BOG 1 to 5. Each group attended a four-day Bank Officers (BO) Knowledge Workshop on customer relations.
- Facilitator Development for the Training Manager - whereby the Training Manager was provided coaching and mentoring in facilitation skills in order to facilitate workshops for the front-line staff.
- Customer Relations Training for the 200 front-line staff – the staff were divided into ten groups of twenty each, called FLG 1 to 10. Each group attended a two-day Front-line (FL) Knowledge Workshop on customer relations skills development.

The BO Knowledge Workshops and the Facilitator Development process for the Training Manager occurred simultaneously in Cycle 1 as shown in Figure 1.9.

Customer Relations Training for Bank Officers

The 60 bank officers were divided into five groups of twelve each, called BOG 1 to 5. Each group attended a four-day Bank Officers (BO) Knowledge Workshop on customer relations.

During the BO Knowledge Workshop for BOG 1, the twelve bank officers acquired knowledge in Customer Relations to improve their own effectiveness. Then, as a team, they used the newly learnt concepts to undertake a work-based project, namely, to develop a draft Customer Relations Guide for the front-line staff who deal with customers.

The bank officers worked as two teams of six to apply the concept of customer relations both for their own individual effectiveness and in the development of the draft Customer Relations Guide. There was a need for two Facilitative Consultants on the program because separate coaching was necessary for the two teams as they completed their draft Customer Relations Guide.

Both teams then shared their drafts with each other in a reflective session. They then reviewed the commonalities and differences and developed what they believed would be an ideal Customer Relations Guide. This process was duplicated at the BO Knowledge Workshops for the other four groups, namely BOG 2 to BOG 5, with each group developing a draft Customer Relations Guide for the front-line staff.

Each of the five groups then nominated one member to form a learning team of five officers (Learning Team). This Learning Team reviewed and reflected on the five draft guides developed by the groups and developed a final draft of what they believed would be an ideal Customer Relations Guide for the front-line staff.

Facilitator Development for the Training Manager

Simultaneously with the BO Knowledge Workshops, the Training Manager went through a Facilitator Development process whereby she developed her facilitation skills as follows:

- by observing and reflecting with the Facilitative Consultants on the Knowledge Workshop for BOG 1;
- by being incrementally involved as a co-facilitator at the remaining BO Knowledge Workshops by contributing 10% of the facilitation for BOG 2, 20% for BOG 3, 20% for BOG 4 and 35-40% for BOG 5; and
- by presenting to the Facilitative Consultants, for their feedback, the proposed session plan and all the required material for the FL Knowledge Workshops.

Subsequently, the Facilitative Consultants provided coaching and mentoring to the Training Manager throughout the delivery of the FL Knowledge Workshops.

This Facilitator Development process for the Training Manager provided an ongoing benefit for the bank since the Training Manager could then train new bank officers and other front-line staff as well as deliver other Work-Based Learning workshops. By developing the skills of the Training Manager, the bank was investing in its own future.

Figure 1.9 – Cycle 1 – Parallel Bank Officer Workshops &
Training Manager Development Process

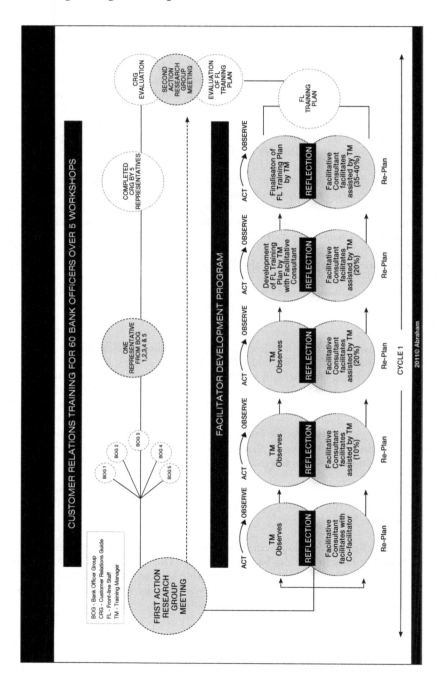

Second AR Group Meeting

From this meeting onwards, the Learning Team became members of the AR Group. At this meeting, the AR Group:

i) reviewed and reflected on the final draft of the Customer Relations Guide which was to be reflected upon by the front-line staff during the FL Knowledge Workshops;
ii) evaluated the session plan and materials developed by the Training Manager for the FL Knowledge Workshops; and
iii) reviewed and commented on the Customer Relations campaign for the branches which had been developed by the Training Manager.

Cycle 2

Customer Relations Training for Front-Line Staff

The 200 front-line staff were divided into ten groups of twenty, namely FLG1 to FLG 20. Each group attended a two-day Knowledge Workshop on customer relations. These ten workshops were facilitated by the Training Manager over a period of five months.

During these workshops, the views of the 200 front-line staff were sought on the final draft Customer Relations Guide, since they were to use the final version as their guide in the workplace. Evaluation of these workshops was undertaken after every workshop and improvements were made to subsequent workshops based on the feedback obtained.

Third AR Group Meeting

At the third AR Group meeting, the members reviewed and analysed the views of the 200 front-line staff on the draft Customer Relations Guide and incorporated these views into the final version of the guide.

They also reviewed the feedback about the workshops and summarised the improvements to be undertaken for future delivery of similar workshops.

The Customer Relations campaign was also finalised for the review of management. Figure 1.10 shows the details of the front-line staff training and the customer relations campaign.

Figure 1.10 – Cycle 2 – Front-Line Staff Training and Customer Relations Campaign

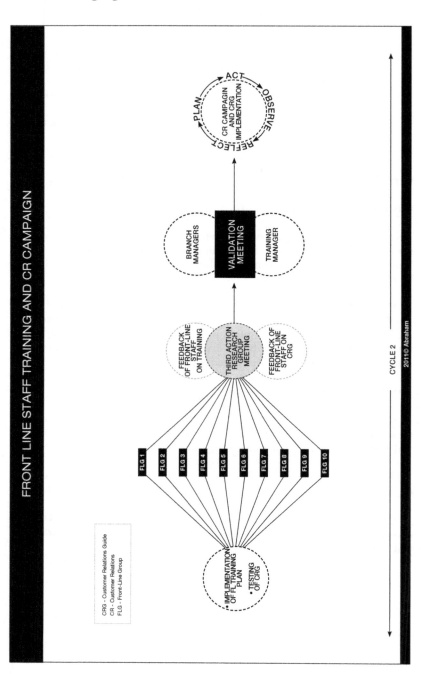

Validation

The Training Manager met with a Validation Committee comprising the branch managers and presented feedback from the following activities for its review and comment:

    i)   the BO Knowledge Workshops
    ii) the Training Manager's Facilitator Development process; and
    iii) the FL Knowledge Workshops

The Training Manager also presented the Customer Relations campaign to the Validation Committee. After incorporation of the views and suggestions of the Validation Committee, the Customer Relations campaign was launched by the Training Manager at the bank branches.

The Validation Committee proposed that at each branch, select bank officers and front-line staff should work as learning teams to monitor and evaluate the performance indicators of project outcomes, learning outcomes and process outcomes.

Another proposal was that each branch should, through a newsletter, share with the other branches lessons learnt from the Customer Relations Program.

CHAPTER SUMMARY

This chapter has described my experiences with WBL and the creation of a WAL model, with case summaries to illustrate the use of the model in different situations.

The next three chapters will further demonstrate how the WAL model has been adapted and used in other WAL programs, whilst still capturing the features of WBL and the ARAL approach.

REFERENCES

Abraham, S, Arnold, G & Oxenberry, R 1996, *The Self-Discovering Organisation: Fusing Action Research to the Learning Organisation*, presented at the conference on "Developing a Learning Organisation through Action Learning and Action Research", 25 & 26 Oct, organised by Action Learning, Action Research & Process Management Association Inc. & Singapore Institute of Management, in Singapore.

Alderman, B, & Milne, P 2005, *A Model for Work-Based Learning*, Scarecrow Press, Lanham, Maryland.

Allen, L 1964, *The Management Profession*, McGraw-Hill Inc., NY, USA.

Argyris, C 1994, 'The Future of Workplace Learning and Performance', Special Supplement, *Training and Development*, May, pp. 36-47.

Australian National Training Authority 1998, *Framing the Future—A Ready Reference*, ANTA, Melbourne.

Bassi, C, Cheney, S & Lewis, E 1998, 'Trends in Workplace Learning: Supply and Demand in interesting times', *Training and Development*, Volume 22, Issue 11, Nov, pp.51-73.

Boud, D & Symes, C 2000, 'Learning for real: work-based education in Universities'. In Symes, C and McIntyre, J (Eds.), *Working Knowledge: The New Vocationalism and Higher Education*, SRHE & Open University Press, Buckingham.

Costley, C 2001, 'Organisational and employee interest sin programs of work based learning', *The Learning Organisation*, Volume 8, Issue 2, pp.58-63.

Fox, S & Grey, C 2000, 'Introduction: Connecting Learning and Critique', *Management Learning*, Volume 31, (1) March, pp. 7-10.

Garnett, J, Costley, C & Workman, B 2009, *Work based learning: journeys to the core of higher education*, Middlesex University Press, London.

Helyer, R 2010, *The Work-based Student Learning Handbook*, Palgrave Macmillan, London.

Jarvis, P, Holford, J & Griffin, C 2003, *The Theory & Practice of Learning*, 2nd Edition, Kogan Page, London.

Lewin, K 1946, 'Action research and Minority Problems', Journal of Social Issues, vol. 2, pp. 34-46, in Kemmis, S & McTaggart, R (Eds.) 1988, *The Action Research Reader*, 3rd ed., Deakin University Press, Melbourne.

Lewin, K 1947, 'Frontiers in Group Dynamics II. Channels of GroupLife, Social Planning and Action Research', *Human Relations*, vol. 1, pp. 143-153.

Lewin, K 1951, *Field Theory in Social Sciences: Selected Theoretical Papers*, Cartwright, D. (Ed.), Harper, New York.

Lewin, K 1952, 'Group Decisions and Social Change', in Swanson, G, Newcombe, T & Hartley E (Eds.), *Readings in Social Psychology*, Henry Holt, New York; and in Kemmis, S & McTaggart, R 1988, *The Action Research Reader*, 3rd ed., Deakin University Press, Melbourne:, pp. 47-56.

Matthews, P 1999, 'Workplace Learning: developing an holistic model', *MCB The Learning Organisation*, Volume 6, Issue 1.

Nichols, F 2000, *Communities of Practice: Definitions, Indicators & Identifying Characteristics*, The Distance Consulting Company, New Jersey.

Peters, M & Robinson, V 1984, 'The Origins and Status of Action Research', *Journal of Applied Behavioural Science*, 20, 2, 113-124

Reddin, W 1970, *Managerial Effectiveness*, McGraw-Hill, NY, USA.

Revans, R 1982, 'What is Action Learning?', *Journal of Management Development*, vol. 1, no. 3, pp. 64-75.

Revans, R 1983, 'Action Learning: Its origins and nature', in Pedler, M (Ed), *Action Learning in Practice*, Gower, Aldershot, Hants.

Raelin, J A 2000, Work-based Learning: The New Frontier of Management Development, Prentice Hall, Upper Saddle River, New Jersey.

Raelin, J 2008, *Work-Based Learning: Bridging Knowledge and Action in the Workplace*, Jossey-Bass, San Francisco.

Resnick, L B 1987, 'Learning in school and out', *Educational Researcher*, 16(9), 13-20.

Resnick, L 1987, *Education and learning to think*, National Academy Press, Washington, DC (ED 289 832).

Roodhouse S & Mumford J 2010, *Understanding work-based learning*, Gower, Surrey.

Ruona, W E A, Lynham, S A and Chemack, T J 2003, 'Insights on Emerging Trends and the Future of Human Resource Development', *Advances in Developing Human Resource*, Volume 5, No. s3, pp. 272-282.

Scribner, S 1986, "Thinking in Action: Some Characteristics of Practical Thought." In Sternberg R J & Wagner R (eds.), *Practical Intelligence: Nature and Origins of Competence*, Cambridge University Press, Cambridge.

Schön D 1983, *The reflective practitioner*, Basic Books, New York.

Tripathi, P & Reddy, P 2007, *Principles of Management*, 3rd ed., Tata McGraw-Hill Publishing, New Delhi, India.

Wallace, G 1926, *The Art of Thought*, J Cape, London.

Watkins, K E & Marsick, V J 1992, 'Towards a theory of informal and incidental learning in organisations', *International Journal of Lifelong Education*, Volume 11, (4), pp. 287-300.

Wenger, E 1999, Communities of *Practice: Learning, Meaning and Identity*, Cambridge University Press, Cambridge.

Wenger, E 2003, 'Interview with Etienne Wenger on Communities of Practice', Knowledge Board: http://www.knowledgeboard.com

Wimmer, R 2011, *The Five Stages of Communication/Persuasion*, http://www.rogerwimmer.com.wrpersuasion.htm

CHAPTER 2

A WORK-APPLIED LEADERSHIP DEVELOPMENT PROGRAM
Colin Brimson

ABSTRACT

The Action Research and Action Learning (ARAL) approach is increasingly being used for leadership and management development. This Work-Applied Learning (WAL) case study reports on the use of an ARAL process in the Delivery Business Unit of Australia Post in South Australia. It shows how an Action Research Group used Action Learning projects within the organisation to develop Delivery Centre Managers and Team Leaders in light of a new organisational structure.

BACKGROUND

Australia Post is a Government Business Enterprise which operates in a competitive commercial environment for the delivery of mail throughout Australia. Apart from the section of the market protected by legislation for letters under 250 grams, it operates competitively in the markets of logistics, retail, and financial services, with its success relying on a staff of 35,000 and a network of 10,000 contractors and agents spread across the whole country.

In 2001, a number of changes were introduced to improve the efficiency of its management and operations. The strategy included a significant investment in training and development. Within the Delivery Business Unit, the change was directed at the establishment of a new Team Leader structure that provided line control. It also required a focus on improving the knowledge and skills of the Delivery Centre Managers who reported, through Area Managers, to the State Manager Delivery (SMD) and the Team Leaders who reported to the Delivery Centre Managers.

This WAL case study documents the design and delivery of a customised program using an ARAL approach developed by Gibaran (currently called the Australian Institute of Business), the SMD for South Australia and the Northern Territory, and his direct reports.

This program was called the Leadership Development Programme.

This WAL case study is presented in three sections. The first section provides a background to the workplace issue that formed the thematic concern of the program. It also examines the reason for using the ARAL approach and sets out the expected outcomes from the Action Learning projects.

The second section presents a reflective narrative summary of the work and learning outcomes that were achieved during the project. The final section considers the characteristics of Action Research that were observed during the course of the program and concludes with an evaluation of the outcomes that were achieved.

PROGRAM BACKGROUND

The issue of training and development was raised following a decision by Australia Post in 1999 to change the organisational structure of its Delivery Centres. The proposed new structure removed existing line control supervisors and replaced them with Team Leaders who would be upgraded and given line control responsibilities for groups of up to twelve Postal Delivery Officers (PDOs).

In a typical Delivery Centre organisation structure before the change, Postal Delivery Controllers had responsibility for the teams of PDOs as shown in Figure 2.1.

Figure 2.1 – Typical Delivery Centre Organisation Chart in SA/NT (before change)

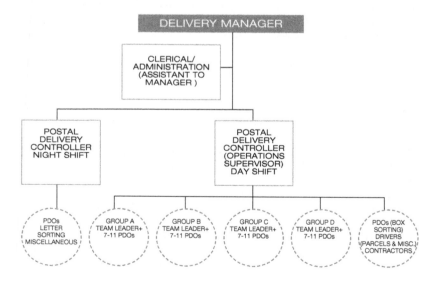

The new structure, in Figure 2.2, shows the Team Leaders taking line management control for the PDOs.

Figure 2.2 – Typical Delivery Centre Organisation Chart in SA/NT (after change)

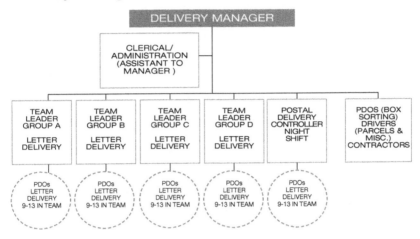

A pilot study program was undertaken during 2000 at one Delivery Centre in each State to test the proposed new structure. During the pilot, it became evident that Delivery Centre Managers in South Australia and the Northern Territory had a significant task to develop up to four Team Leaders per Delivery Centre in the wide range of supervisory tasks and skills that would enable them to effectively fulfil their new role and responsibilities.

This new structure was to be implemented from January 2002 and required major changes in the way Delivery Centres were to operate. Delivery Centre Managers needed help to train and develop their new Team Leaders to become effective line control supervisors.

The traditional way of learning and implementing a major change program would have been to conduct briefings for the Delivery Centre Managers, and to provide them with guidelines for implementation. Team Leaders would be given on-the-job training, and perhaps a few specific classroom-type training sessions. Each Delivery Centre Manager would implement the program using their own style. This fragmented approach would result in varying degrees of individual learning, combined with short-term projects. There was no consistent system for learning and problem solving in Delivery Centres and no integrated approach towards individual and team learning at the different levels and functions in the organisation.

Delivery Centre Managers had differing levels of ability to develop their subordinate staff. Some were naturally good at this and others were quite autocratic in their approach to implementing change and solving problems.

For several years, the SMD had thought that there was a better way to train and develop his people; however, this was a matter that seemed to be solely within the control of the Human Resource Department. It was not until after his promotion to the position of State Manager Delivery, and commencement of his MBA studies, that the SMD gave consideration to the introduction of an Action Learning development program. This was brought about by a clearly identified need to train and develop Delivery Centre Managers and Team Leaders and a desire to improve the way in which people learn and implement change programs.

Quite simply, there had to be a better way than the traditional way, and it seemed from his own learning that ARAL could be a more powerful method of learning that would also produce better business outcomes. Now he was in a position to implement a leadership development program as part of his MBA studies, and as a researcher, to test the ARAL approach on a real need within the workplace. This led to an investigation into the possible implementation of a Leadership Development Program, initially for the Delivery Centre Managers and then for the Team Leaders, using the ARAL approach.

Just as there is no right recipe for success in organisational terms, there is no "right" way to develop people. This program was initiated by the SMD as researcher because of his involvement in Action Learning as part of his MBA studies at Gibaran and a desire to change and improve the way Australia Post employees learn in the Delivery Business Unit of South Australia. In addition, there was a need for Delivery Centre Managers to develop their subordinate Team Leaders, following a structural change in the organisation.

THE ACTION RESEARCH QUESTIONS AND DESIRED OUTCOMES

The workplace challenges in developing Delivery Centre Managers and Team Leaders were incorporated into the Leadership Development Program and the SMD's MBA Action Research Project.

A number of questions were posed to address the workplace challenges in developing Delivery Centre Managers and Team Leaders using ARAL:

(i) What was the Action Research and Action Learning (ARAL) model that emerged from the program?
(ii) What were the Action Research characteristics that emerged from the program?

(iii) What were the projects that were implemented using the Action Learning approach?

(iv) Were the projects beneficial to the Delivery Business Unit?

(v) If ARAL was not used during this program, would the Delivery Business Unit have achieved the same project outcomes?

(vi) What were the lessons learned by the SMD as researcher?

Answers to these questions were sought during the implementation of the new structure for the Delivery Business Unit, and the SMD had some specific desired outcomes in mind when the program commenced, as outlined below:

1. Develop a skilled and motivated leadership team in all large Delivery Centres within 12-18 months;

2. Involve all Delivery Centre Managers in the learning process, and have this become a normal way of operating in the Delivery Business Unit in South Australia & Northern Territory;

3. Delivery Centre Managers to have enhanced facilitation and coaching skills;

4. Team Leaders to have a clear understanding of their new role and responsibilities;

5. Team Leaders to have a clear understanding of how their role and responsibilities link to national, state and business unit goals and objectives;

6. Team Leaders to adopt Action Learning as a way of solving problems and making improvements within work teams in Delivery Centres;

7. Improved customer service quality and productivity to be achieved with letter deliveries in metropolitan Delivery Centres;

8. An increased understanding of organisational learning and the benefits of developing a learning organisation culture in Australia Post; and

9. Implementation of a continuous learning culture throughout all Delivery Business units in South Australia and the Northern Territory.

These desired outcomes were shared with all Delivery Centre Managers who participated in the early part of the program, and were reflected on during the later stages of the program.

WHY ACTION RESEARCH AND ACTION LEARNING (ARAL)?

The social psychologist Kurt Lewin (1890-1947) developed and applied the concept of Action Research over a number of years in a series of community experiments in post-World War II America.

Two of the concepts which were crucial in Lewin's work were the ideas of group decision and commitment to improvement (Kemmis and McTaggart

1988). Although Lewin did not define the processes of Action Research, he indicated that Action Research Group members should:

(i) develop a plan of critically informed action to improve what is already happening;

(ii) act to implement the plan;

(iii) observe the effects of the critically informed action in the context in which it occurs; and

(iv) reflect on these effects as a basis for further planning, subsequent critically informed action and so on, through a succession of cycles.

The ARAL model that emerged from this program relates to the four-stage process outlined by Lewin. Firstly, a plan to improve leadership qualities for Australia Post Delivery Centre Managers and Team Leaders was developed by an Action Research Group made up of the SMD, the Gibaran Facilitator, three Area Managers and three representative Delivery Centre Managers within the Delivery Business Unit.

Information on the Leadership Development Program, Action Research and Action Learning was obtained from relevant literature and other sources, both on and off the job.

Next, the plan was implemented with all Delivery Centre Managers attending the Knowledge Workshops of the Leadership Development Program at Gibaran to receive knowledge on leadership related subjects. During the Work-Based Phases between the Knowledge Workshops, they applied their learning by way of project work on the job. The Delivery Centre Managers applied the concept of Action Learning and facilitated their projects with others directly affected at Delivery Centre level.

At the third stage, the Action Research Group met to reflect on events and learning, after each Knowledge Workshop at Gibaran.

Finally, the plan was reviewed by the Action Research Group with appropriate adjustment to improve benefits of the program as it progressed. The application of these ARAL elements can be seen in the model in Figure 2.3.

Figure 2.3 – Australia Post Delivery Business (SA/NT)
Integrated Action Research - Action Learning (ARAL) Model

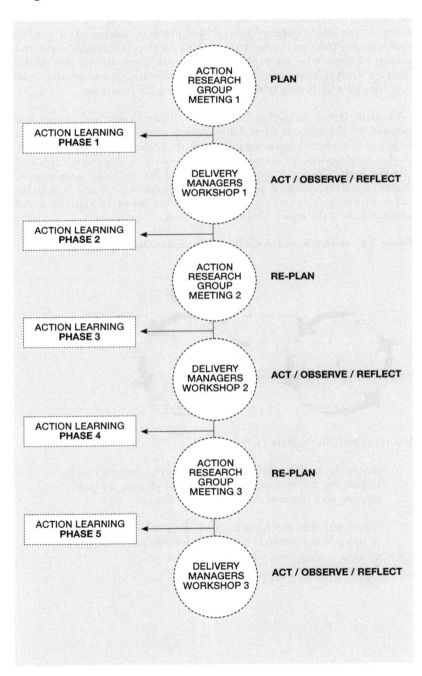

The Action Research method is described by Cunningham (1993) as "a continuous process of research and learning in the researcher's and the group's long-term relationship with a problem". Action Research encouraged the SMD (the researcher) to experience the problem as it evolved. This is the action of "engaging" in real life problem solving, and getting legitimisation from real organisations. This requires the commitment and interest of those who are experiencing the problems. In the case of the Delivery Centre Managers, the Knowledge Workshops and project work were relevant and directly related to real working life situations.

Abraham (1994) said that "the Action Research method is problem focussed in the context of real life situations and the solving of such problems in a research sense would benefit the organisation and contribute to the development of social science knowledge". Abraham explained that the Action Research method, when used for the implementation of change, involves cycles of planning, action, observation and reflection, and re-planning. The ongoing process cycles are shown in Figure 2.4 and continued until the conclusion of the program.

Figure 2.4 – Action Research Cycles for Implementation of Change

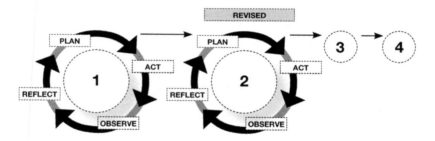

According to Cunningham (1993):

> Action Research is a process where employees become jointly responsible for managing the process of change through a steering committee or Action Research Group;

> before Action Research can begin, there must be an acceptance of its goals and methods as well as a positive and cooperative attitude among those who are carrying it out.

People cannot make intelligent choices about Action Research techniques unless they feel competent to deal with the problems of other people, and the best way to train the Action Research Group is by practical application (Cunningham 1993). In this case, the program was led by the SMD (researcher), the most senior functional manager for the Delivery Business Unit, and he was able to authorise the use of resources to successfully complete the program. In addition, the most senior state manager endorsed the program.

The Action Research Group (Table 2.1 lists the members) met on regular occasions to discuss issues that surfaced during the implementation of the plan, and to ensure learning sessions covered any gaps in the process. The SMD (as researcher) was involved in the process and was supported by Area Managers who were also doing project work with Delivery Centre Managers.

Table 2.1 – Action Research Group Members

The Action Research Group comprised the following members:
- Colin Brimson, the State Manager Delivery, an MBA student and initiator of the change program;
- the Southern Area Manager, who usually acted as State Manager Delivery in the absence of Colin Brimson;
- the Eastern Area Manager;
- the Northern Area Manager;
- the Glynde Delivery Centre Manager, who usually acted as the Eastern Area Manager in his absence;
- the Port Adelaide Delivery Centre Manager;
- the Somerton Park Delivery Centre Manager, who usually acted as Southern Area Manager in his absence.
- Chris Riley, the Gibaran Consultant and Facilitator of the Leadership Development Program.

Others were invited to meet with the group as required.

The model in Figure 2.5 shows the relationships between the Action Research Group, Area Managers and Delivery Centre Managers (DCM).

Figure 2.5 – Action Research Group Relationships

THE LEADERSHIP DEVELOPMENT PROGRAM

Delivery Centres vary in size and have between two and four Team Leaders, and up to twelve Postal Delivery Officers in each team. The effect of the structural change on the Team Leaders in the Delivery Centres was that they had to be trained and developed to take on first-line managerial responsibilities. The Leadership Development Program included the development of Delivery Centre Managers as well as the training of the Team Leaders. It was structured into two tiers and delivered in several phases.

The Phase 1 intervention involved the SMD (researcher) working with Gibaran to customise the Leadership Development Program for Delivery Centre Managers and their Team Leaders. In the first phase, Delivery Centre Managers were introduced to the principles and practices of Action Learning, Leadership, Strategic Operations and the facilitation of workplace projects.

The Phase 2 intervention involved the development of Team Leaders. This was undertaken through an internal Australia Post program, and an accredited Certificate IV in Front-line Management program at Gibaran that incorporated the principles and practices of Action Learning. The participants in each intake of the Certificate IV program consisted of one Team Leader from each of the Delivery Centres. This was to ensure that every Delivery Centre Manager had at least one Team Leader who had an understanding of Action Learning principles and was able to facilitate a team working on a real problem in the workplace.

The Phase 3 intervention of the program involved Area Managers and Delivery Centre Managers in continuing to develop their skills at Gibaran, gaining an accredited Graduate Certificate in Management qualification on successful completion of the Leadership Development Program, and cascading the facilitation of Action Learning projects throughout the Delivery Business Units in South Australia and the Northern Territory.

THE ACTION LEARNING PROJECTS

The Action Learning projects were linked to the Delivery Business Unit plan to improve customer service quality and productivity. Area Managers had a key role in driving improvements as each one embraced the concept of Action Learning. All Delivery Centre Managers and Team Leaders in the Leadership Development Program were required to undertake projects linked to service quality or productivity improvement, and the initial projects formed the basis on which learning would take place in the long term. Team Leaders would later undertake a Certificate IV in Frontline Management program at Gibaran, also embracing the Action Learning concept by working through projects on the job. Hence the first model (Figure 2.5) can be expanded to show the proposed learning sets at the next two levels, as illustrated in Figure 2.6.

Figure 2.6 – Second and Third Level Action Learning Groups

(1) Delivery Centre Managers with Team Leaders and key staff
(2) Team Leaders (TL) with Postal Delivery Officers (PDOs)

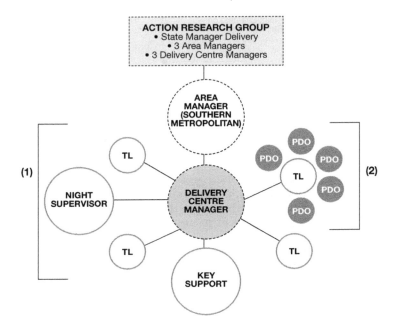

Planning for each phase of the program was done by the Action Research Group. All members of the Action Research Group participated in the Leadership Development Program, and the SMD (researcher) co-facilitated the program, which had been specifically tailored towards the business needs of the Delivery Business Unit. After each Knowledge Workshop, the Action Research Group met to discuss outcomes, share observations and reflect on implementation of the plan.

Each Action Research Group member was allocated tasks and was required to bring knowledge back to the group throughout the program. Special guests and participants were invited to join the Action Research Group, make presentations and provide feedback. The Leadership Development Program for the Delivery Business Unit was thus an integrated Action Research and Action Learning (ARAL) program. The various phases and learning groups in the ARAL program are shown in Figure 2.7.

Figure 2.7 – Leadership Development Program for Delivery Business Unit in SA/NT using Action Research and Action Learning

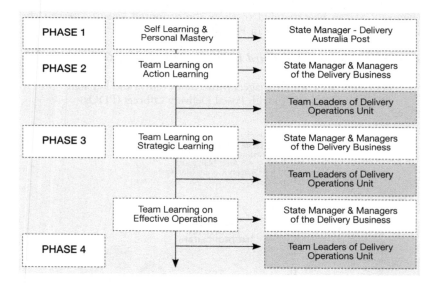

The program effectively started with the SMD's (researcher's) own learning whilst undertaking MBA studies. This was followed by the Delivery Centre Managers being given the opportunity to undertake a Graduate Certificate in Management program.

One Team Leader from each Delivery Centre then commenced a Certificate IV in Frontline Management program. Phases 4 and beyond represent the continuing programs for new cohorts of Team Leaders from the Delivery Centres.

ACTION RESEARCH - ACTION LEARNING WORK AND LEARNING OUTCOMES

The SMD was closely involved in all stages of the learning and development programs and kept a record of the activities of the Leadership Development Program for the Delivery Centre Managers and the Certificate IV in Frontline Management Program for the Team Leaders.

A list of the individual Action Learning projects and their outcomes is shown in Tables 2.2 and 2.3.

Table 2.2 – Delivery Centre Managers' Projects and Performance Outcomes

PARTICIPANT	PROJECT DESCRIPTION	OUTCOMES
Manager Lonsdale DC	Matching labour resources to workload for street mail delivery function.	• Improved productivity (not specified) and customer service • Balanced workloads – improved morale • Structure and process for learning and change implemented • Team Leaders learning
Manager O'Halloran Hill DC	Understanding cost drivers at O'Halloran Hill and reducing operating costs.	• Clear understanding of costs – team learning • Operational savings realised
Manager Somerton Park DC	Improving customer service in the Somerton Park delivery area and improving internal cross functional relationships.	• Redirection complaints reduced • Incorrect Delivery complaints reduced • Retail / Licensee / Delivery and Transport relationships improved • Operational savings realised
Manager Marleston DC	Improving on-time service for business customers in the Marleston area, and enhancing flexibility of resources.	• Service standards improved • Operational savings realised • Team learning • Structure and process to resolve issues and implement change

Table 2.2 – Delivery Centre Managers' Projects and Performance Outcomes (contd.)

PARTICIPANT	PROJECT DESCRIPTION	OUTCOMES
Manager Regency Park DC	Improving the workplace environment and mail processing activities at Regency Park Delivery Centre.	• Level of mis-sorted mail reduced • Changed housekeeping culture to maintain tidy work areas • Reduced costs (unspecified) to service Retail Shops in area
Manager Port Adelaide DC	Better management of staff on restricted duties due to injury or illness at Port Adelaide.	• Limitations of all affected staff reviewed • Specific duty statements and job descriptions issued • Improved productivity (not specified) and morale
Manager Salisbury South DC	Reducing the amount of rework at Salisbury South associated with receipt of mis-sorted mail.	• Reduced level of mis-sorted mail • Operational savings realised • Enhanced continuous improvement culture
Manager Elizabeth West DC	Improving quality customer service at Elizabeth by reducing mail redirection errors.	• Redirection failures reduced • Cost reduction (not specified) • Improved customer satisfaction
Manager Modbury North DC	Effective utilisation of staff that are ill or injured in the workplace.	• Attendance improved • Productivity improved • Operational savings realised • Morale improved
Manager Melrose Park DC	Review of labour utilised to meet workload.	• Staff workloads balanced • Operational savings realised • Improved service to business customers • Team learning

Table 2.2 – Delivery Centre Managers' Projects and Performance Outcomes (contd.)

PARTICIPANT	PROJECT DESCRIPTION	OUTCOMES
Manager Glynde DC	Alignment of labour to workloads and improvement of customer service.	• Operational savings realised • Attendance improved • Service to business community improved delivery on time • Redirection failures and incorrect deliveries reduced
Manager Unley DC	Improving productivity and service to business customers in the Unley Delivery area.	• Service to private boxes improved • Customer complaints reduced • No increase in labour utilisation • Manager and Team Leaders learning • Improved morale
Manager Address POST Unit	Review of Australia Post's Mail Redirection System with recommendations that will reduce customer failures.	• Data gathered and analysed • Root causes identified (4 key areas) • Recommendations made (State and HQ)
Area Manager Southern	Improving leadership in Delivery Centres by assessing needs for Team Leaders, developing and implementing internal and external training programs.	• Audit undertaken to assess Team Leaders' training needs • Three internal training modules developed and conducted • External program arranged to improve communication skills of all Team Leaders • Structure and process for Managers to deal with problems and change • Team Leaders learning
Area Manager Northern	Reduce the number of lost time injuries and more effectively rehabilitate injured employees.	• Compensation claims reduced • Compensation costs reduced • Managers more knowledgeable about Compensation and Rehabilitation Act

Table 2.3 – Team Leader Certificate IV Program – Projects &
Performance Outcomes

PARTICIPANT	PROJECT DESCRIPTION	OUTCOMES
Acting Team Leader Lonsdale DC	Improving letterbox provision and placements in area.	• Reduced safety risk • Improved productivity • Quality Customer Service (QCS) improvement
Team Leader O'Halloran Hill DC	Improving letterbox provision and placements in team area.	• Reduced safety risk • Improved productivity • QCS improvement
Team Leader Somerton Park DC	Improving team performance.	• Improved productivity • QCS improvement
Team Leader Marleston DC	Improving letterbox provision and placements in team area.	• Reduced safety risk • Improved productivity • QCS improvement
Team Leader Regency Park DC	Reducing the level of mis-sorted mail and re-work at Regency Park Delivery Centre.	• QCS improvement • Improved productivity
Team Leader Port Adelaide DC	Customer Commitments and a Review of Response Procedures.	• QCS improvement • Reduced re-work • Improved productivity
Team Leader Salisbury South DC	Conduct a review of delivery arrangements in the Salisbury 'Evens' group, to include the provision of deliveries to new housing development in the area.	• QCS improvement • improved productivity • improved cost effectiveness
Team Leader Elizabeth West DC	Improved safe working practices at Elizabeth West Delivery Centre.	• QCS improvement • Improved productivity • Cost reduction
Team Leader Modbury North DC	Improving letterbox provision and placements in area.	• Reduced safety risk • Improved productivity • QCS improvement

Table 2.3 – Team Leader Certificate IV Program – Projects &
Performance Outcomes (contd.)

PARTICIPANT	PROJECT DESCRIPTION	OUTCOMES
Team Leader Kent Town DC	Improve utilisation of staffing arrangements including relief arrangements and delivery round splits.	• Reduced HR usage • Dollar savings • Improved customer service • Improved productivity
Team Leader Glynde DC	Improve utilisation of staffing arrangements including relief arrangements and splits.	• Reduced HR usage • $dollar savings • QCS improvement • Productivity improvement
Team Leader Unley DC	Develop Quality Action System for Relief staff.	• Improved customer service, internal & external • Reduced rework • Quality control measures in place

REFLECTIONS AND INSIGHTS INTO THE WORKINGS OF ARAL

Observations of the activities of the Action Research Group by the Delivery Centre Managers and Team Leaders during the course of the program provide reflection and insights into the workings of the ARAL method and are presented in this section.

11 Sep Year 1   Initial discussions at Gibaran considered a proposed general framework for the Action Research Project and the development of a "customised" Leadership Development Program (LDP) for Delivery Centre Managers (DCMs). Possible members of the Action Research Group (ARG) included three Area Managers, three DCMs (one from each network) and the Delivery Training Coordinator. It was not known at this stage what level of support would be provided by the General Manager.

26 Sep Year 1   At a meeting with the Area Managers and the Delivery Training Coordinator the broad plan for developing DCMs and Team Leaders, using Action Learning was presented. It involved the formation of a review team (later to become an Action Research Group), which included the Area Managers and one key DCM from each network. The review team's role was to assist the DCMs on a "continuous improvement" journey, starting with implementation of the new delivery structure. It was emphasised that DCMs had to change the way they operated and would be required to train and develop Team Leaders in their new role. All Area Managers were asked to present the plan to the DCMs and provide feedback. They were required to explain the role of the review team and to consider the nomination of a "key" DCM per network.

3 Oct Year 1   The plan for the development of DCMs and Team Leaders was presented to the Delivery Business Unit Manager. He gave his full support and suggested that the plan be presented to the entire Mail and Networks Management Team for SA/NT and a presentation made to the National Manager. During the presentation, the National Manager had questions relating to measurable outcomes and gave his support for the program.

11 Oct Year 1   The ARG met and considered progress made with the Delivery Centre modelling exercise. This was an exercise designed to clarify the tasks Team Leaders were required to carry out, and how much time was needed to do the work. A national team comprising members from Australia Post management and the Communications, Electrical and Plumbers Union (CEPU) was responsible for the review and its recommendations. The placement of Delivery Operations Support staff was considered along with Team Leaders who were to be moved into the new higher - graded positions. The Leadership Development Program Plan and the role of the ARG were reviewed, with one of the DCMs offering to bring a videotape on team development to the ARG meeting.

16 Oct Year   At an ARG meeting, the SMD provided an update on the Leadership Development Program (LDP). He introduced the Gibaran Facilitator who explained the concept of Action Learning, the methodology and associated formulae, including Work-Based Learning (WBL) = PK + PQ (Work- Based Learning includes Programmed Knowledge and Questioning Insight applied to a real work Project). It was agreed that the ARG members would submit their thoughts about suitable projects to the SMD, for further discussion at the next meeting.

24 Oct Year 1   Day 1 of the LDP started with an explanation of Action Learning, followed by a videotape and discussion on the importance of having a vision for the organisation. Small groups were formed to consider appropriate project topics and these ideas were presented for further discussion by the entire group. The SMD presented his "desired outcomes" to the group. One of the DCMs said that it was all "mumbo jumbo" and other participants expressed their uncertainty about some of the "project" issues. These concerns were addressed with further clarification of the Action Learning processes to be used in the projects.

1 Nov Year 1   Day 2 of LDP started with reflections on Day 1 and led to discussion about leadership styles. The ARAL model was presented (Figure 2.3) to show how Action Learning teams and the ARG would operate. The SMD spoke about the process of problem solving and implementing change programs using Action Learning groups, with managers facilitating projects.

The groups then discussed potential projects and considered the development of project plans. All agreed that projects must relate to the key issues of improving customer service, productivity, the training and development of Team Leaders, or a combination of these. Explanation was provided for participants on how they could use their LDP projects to help obtain a Graduate Certificate in Management qualification.

7 Nov Year 1   The ARG met to review Days 1 and 2 of the LDP and discuss Day 3's content. The training needs for Team Leaders was discussed and it was agreed that the Training Co-ordinator would develop a training matrix for identification of required training modules. It was emphasised that all DCMs needed to provide on-the-job training as soon as possible, and not wait for an internal program to be established.

Although the Action Learning articles initially caused some confusion for DCMs, the facilitator explained that this was not unusual in the early stages of the program. The DCMs now had a better understanding of an ARG member's role, with sharing tasks and information gathering.

22 Nov Year 1   On Day 3 of the LDP, each DCM gave an update on their activities, including how they approached set members and how they decided on their project topic. Several DCMs still seemed unsure about the concept of Action Learning and how it linked to their project. This day's program included a telephone call from the State Secretary of the CEPU indicating that the projects had not involved consultation with the CEPU. The group used this development to discuss the issue of working with the Union and keeping them informed of developments so that they could better understand and support the program.

29 Nov Year 1   The ARG reviewed program activities and agreed to invite the CEPU Secretary to join one of the sessions. ARG member observations and reflection indicated that the LDP was moving along well, with less anxiety and greater participant understanding of how working on a project was part of Action Learning.

10 Dec Year 1   The CEPU Secretary and the Industrial Officer were invited to provide input into the development of a Team Leader training program. The CEPU Secretary accepted the invitation to attend one of the workshops to show his support and to talk about effective consultation between DCMs and the CEPU.

10 Jan Year 2   The ARG meeting included two DCMs who had been trialling the new organisational structure in their facilities. The State Training Co-ordinator also attended to develop a training program for Team Leaders that would help them fulfil their new role in a revised Delivery Centre structure. Issues from the trials included re-organising rounds, delegating tasks and building the confidence of Team Leaders. The ARG reflected on identified needs and developed an outline of internal and external training.

Internal training was to focus on (a) technical knowledge; (b) people leadership; (c) quality customer service; (d) injury prevention; (e) injury management; (f) basic financial analysis; and (g) key performance indicators.

External training was to focus on personal development in the competencies covered within the Certificate IV in Frontline Management qualification.

25 Jan Year 2 The ARG Meeting agreed to assist in the development of six internal training modules, and this training would run concurrently with the Certificate IV in Frontline Management program at Gibaran. The design would engage DCMs and their Team Leaders in Action Learning projects.

31 Jan Year 2 Day 4 of the LDP reviewed what the DCMs had learned from the Action Learning literature they had been given at the previous workshop. Some had read the articles but with varying degrees of understanding. All of the DCMs were provided with a copy of Weinstein's (1995) book on Action Learning. When reporting the progress on project activities, most said that they were progressing well, but there were some exceptions. One DCM was having difficulty getting a team together and another was extremely frustrated and unsure of how he was going.

These concerns were discussed and considered as a group. The willingness of the DCMs to share their problems enabled different levels of learning with and from each other. The frustrated DCM proved to be a good barometer on the progress of the program because he was always frank and open with his thoughts. He was open to receiving advice from others and those who knew his style of working recognised that his approach was one of doing, rather than delegating responsibility and authority.

27 Feb Year 2 The ARG reviewed developments with the design of the Team Leaders' internal training program and group members were allocated tasks to assist in completing the detailed content for each session.

28 Feb Year 2 Day 5 of the LDP revealed a number of issues with the progress of projects and associated learning. Finding time for the projects was considered a problem for one DCM. Another worked in a different structure with a cross-functional team that did not report to him directly, and this required the use of a different set of management skills.

The Action Learning method was considered too slow by one of the DCMs, whereas another had completely misunderstood the difference between facilitating his project and past projects.

His reaction, after reading the Weinstein text on Action Learning, was to expand the scope of the project to achieve better work and learning outcomes.

The CEPU Secretary joined this session and shared his knowledge about consultation, communication and developing trust in the workplace. This was followed with a discussion about the development of Team Leaders and CEPU support in their new role.

18 Mar Year 2   ARG meetings now included more questions about the programs, about learning and also on how to improve in the future. One of the Area Managers noted that the current approach to learning was quite the reverse of Australia Post's traditional approach to achieving change of direction.

26 Mar Year 2   The SMD welcomed the group to Day 1 of the Team Leaders Certificate IV Program. He was one of the facilitators for the session and each day there would be at least one DCM present as a facilitator. The Team Leaders were given an outline of the Certificate IV program and how it linked with the LDP. They learnt about the Action Learning projects to be undertaken in their Delivery Centres and spent some time discussing potential project topics and the issues that Team Leaders confronted in the workplace.

27 Mar Year 2   During Day 6 of the LDP, the SMD shared his desired outcomes from the program and answered questions about the project presentations that were to be delivered to Australia Post's General Manager and State Mails Manager. It was decided that a PowerPoint template would be provided for the DCMs to use in delivering their reports. The DCMs would also be given the opportunity to make one or two practice presentations before the final presentation.

12 Apr Year 2   The ARG reported on the feedback obtained from Team Leaders about their introduction day. Various degrees of confidence and fear were noted, along with concerns about using a computer to write assignments. The SMD provided information on a communication training package available through Mission Australia that provides basic computer skills training. The ARG decided that each member would attend one day of that program and report back to the ARG meetings.

2 May Year 2   Presentation skills were covered on Day 7 of the LDP. While a few of the DCMs had produced draft PowerPoint presentations, in this session all of the DCMs delivered a report using notes and the whiteboard. They each received feedback and tips on how to improve their presentations and it was agreed that a final practice session would be arranged before the formal presentations to the Australia Post General Manager and State Mails Manager. One of the most outstanding reports was from the DCM who had initially described the Action Learning process as "mumbo jumbo". The presentation highlighted his early frustrations and how much he had learned from his participation in the program.

5-7 Jul Year 2   Over these three days, the DCMs presented their PowerPoint reports to the General Manager and State Mails Manager for Australia Post. This timeframe was required because of the numbers involved. The General Manager was most impressed with the learning and outcomes of the projects, and the structure and process that had been introduced to the Delivery Business Unit. He said that the Delivery Business Unit in South Australia was well placed to lead change and manage issues confronting the business, and most likely better prepared than other States. The SMD expressed his thanks and congratulated the DCMs on their achievements. They were reminded that this was not the end of the learning journey but that Action Learning would continue to be an integral part of their working life.

ACTION RESEARCH CHARACTERISTICS OBSERVED IN THE PROJECT

Abraham (1996) lists twelve characteristics as benchmarks for understanding Action Research. An analysis of these shows that a majority of the elements that define an Action Research Project were evident in the Leadership Development Program for DCMs.

1. Problem focus characteristic
The Action Research method is problem focused in the context of real life situations and the solving of such problems in a research sense would contribute to the practice and the development of social science knowledge.

A real training problem existed for the Delivery Business Unit whereby a change to the structure of the organisation required rapid development of

Team Leaders to equip them for their new responsibilities. First, however, there was a need to develop the leadership skills of the DCMs.

2. Action orientation characteristic
The diagnosis of a problem and the development of a plan can only be considered to be action oriented if it becomes part of a process to implement the plan. This brings an action element to the solving of an immediate problem of the organisation which has strategic change implications for the organisation.

An Action Research Group was formed to solve a problem that required significant change in the way learning and development occurred for the Australia Post Delivery Business Unit in South Australia.

3. Cyclical process: spiral of steps
The Action Research method involves cycles of planning, action, observation, and reflection (evaluation). Also the cycles of the Action Research method allow the group members to develop a plan, to act, to observe and to reflect on this plan and to modify this plan based on the needs of the group members and the requirements of the organisation and situation. A record of the processes of each cycle enables its strengths and weaknesses to be reviewed so that modifications and strategies can be developed for future cycles.

The cycle of steps as described by Abraham (1997) are evident in the Delivery Business Unit Leadership Development Program for Delivery Managers, because Action Learning programs were designed, monitored and adjusted as a result of observation and reflection by the Action Research Group.

4. Collaborative characteristic
Collaboration is a fundamental ingredient of the Action Research method, because without this team effort to solve problems in an environment of participation, Action Research cannot exist. Collaboration on group problems using the Action Research method can be viewed as a continuum from total dependence on the facilitator, who acts as a leader directing the group problem solving process, through to the total management of the problem by the group members, with the facilitator acting as a resource person. The position of the facilitator and the group on this continuum depends on the situation and the needs of the group.

Collaboration occurred between members of the Action Research Group, that included co-facilitators, one external to the company and the other being the researcher. There was an element of self-managing as the group held two meetings in the absence of both co-facilitators during the project.

5. Ethical basis characteristic
Community interests, improvements in the lives of the group members, justice, rationality, democracy and equality are some of the themes of 'ethical' behaviour. The ethical basis of Action Research is an important characteristic to consider, because the Action Research method involves to a

large extent, groups of people with limited power who are open to exploitation. It behooves the researcher to compromise his or her personal needs so that the needs of the group are given the highest priority.

Certainly a degree of democracy and equality was evident during the Leadership Development Program. All members of the Action Research Group had input and all decisions were put to the group for consensus or at least majority agreement. Outcomes of the ARAL project have provided benefits to group members' working lives.

6. Experimental characteristic
Experimental Action Research involves the rigorous testing of hypotheses and can thus contribute to knowledge in social science. Nevertheless, the quality of the Action Research may be affected by the control group which can lead to other problems and complications.

This characteristic did not emerge during the programme, although a number of questions were posed in the early stages.

7. Scientific characteristic
Since the Action Research method does have a scientific basis and can provide an alternative to the positivistic view of science, it is essential that the research be conducted in such a way as to defend itself against criticisms of lack of scientific rigour.

Members of the Action Research Group kept diary notes. Discussions were held with the DCMs during the program. Audit on the effectiveness of the DCMs on-the-job before commencement and during the program occurred. Discussions with selected senior management and Union leaders occurred, with feedback, and in the case of the Union they provided some input to the program. Use of this triangulation technique gives more credibility to the program as data from various sources on the same subject can be compared. Documents relating to the program were kept in both hard copy and electronic form.

8. Re-educative characteristic
Action research can be viewed as re-educative, since it contributes to a change in the knowledge base of the client organisation, a change in the skills, attitudes and knowledge of the individual group members and a change in the skills and knowledge of the researcher. It also makes a contribution to several of the social sciences.

All participants developed their facilitation skills and become more effective in developing their subordinate staff. A new structure and process for problem solving and implementing change has been introduced to Australia Post's delivery facilities in the metropolitan area of Adelaide.

9. Emancipatory characteristic

The Action Research method includes an emancipatory characteristic which will result in some improvements in the lives of the people involved in the Action Research Project, and may also lead to wider social action and reform.

Approximately half of the participants in the programme elected to work towards gaining a Graduate Certificate in Management, and a few of these continued their formal learning to acquire an MBA qualification. Evidence demonstrated that learning during the program had a positive effect on the working lives of DCMs. The process required use of their facilitation, coaching and delegation skills, and this resulted in faster learning by Team Leaders. One DCM commented that his Team Leaders were 50% more effective than he thought they were going to be at that stage of the program.

10. Naturalistic characteristic

If one accepts that Action Research should be scientific but that there are problems in adopting a positivistic model of science and applying it to social science settings, then it follows that a naturalistic approach is appropriate for the Action Research method. The approach involves qualitative descriptions recorded as case studies rather than laws of cause and effect tested experimentally with statistical analysis of data.

The whole process was quite natural, in that participants continued to work at their normal times and worked on projects that were required as part of their leadership role and responsibilities.

11. Normative characteristic

The normative characteristic of Action Research implies that the social 'norms' of the group are not only considered during the research, but, in order to bring about change in the group, they are modified during the Action Research process.

All participants learned the skill of reflection and in the early stages of the program commented that this was one area previously given less time than desired. In the latter stages, it was evident that reflection had become a normal part of the process, as did observation during plan implementation.

12. Group dynamics characteristic

The success of the Action Research method will depend on how well the group can operate as an effective team. An understanding of group dynamics therefore seems essential in facilitating this process and dealing with problems that arise during the Action Research cycles.

Good teamwork existed during the program. All problems encountered were discussed and participants re-planned and took action to overcome such problems. Participation in the Action Research Group, the Action Learning Projects and the workshop sessions at Gibaran provided many opportunities for observing, reflecting upon and learning about team dynamics.

Evaluation of outcomes achieved

Management development programs have traditionally been designed by Human Resource Managers with little input from those actually involved in the program, and limited involvement by operational managers. In addition, training and development programs have traditionally been aimed at individual learning, rather than group learning, and they have seldom been linked directly to company goals and objectives.

At the outset of this case study, the SMD developed measurable outcomes that were referred to as "desirable outcomes". At the time of writing the summary report, some progress had been made towards achieving the desirable outcomes and these are summarised in Table 2.4.

Table 2.4 – Evaluation of Outcomes Achieved

	SMD'S DESIRABLE OUTCOMES	COMMENTS / RESULTS AT TIME OF WRITING
1.	To have a skilled Delivery leadership team within 12-18 months.	DCMs and Team Leaders have improved their leadership skills during the program, and results have been most encouraging. Research has shown that leadership development is a slow process and more time may be required to reach desired levels of competency.
2.	Involve all Delivery Centre Managers in the learning process, and have this become a normal way of operating in the Delivery Business Unit in SA/NT.	The Action Research Group continues to meet on a regular basis to discuss all matters pertaining to learning and leadership.
3.	DCMs to have enhanced facilitation and coaching skills.	Outcomes from phase one of the program were very good and evidenced that facilitation and coaching skills were enhanced.
4.	Team Leaders to have a clear understanding of their new role and responsibilities.	An audit has revealed that a majority of Team Leaders have a sound understanding of their role and responsibilities.

Table 2.4 – Evaluation of Outcomes Achieved (contd.)

	SMD'S DESIRABLE OUTCOMES	COMMENTS / RESULTS AT TIME OF WRITING
5.	Team Leaders to have a clear understanding of how their role and responsibilities link to national, state and business unit goals and objectives.	Special presentations occur each year as the national and state plans are communicated to all staff and implemented. Team Leaders understand this and their role and responsibilities.
6.	Team Leaders adopt Action Learning as a way of solving problems and making improvements within work teams in the Delivery Business unit.	The special audit has shown that only a small number of Team Leaders have adopted an Action Learning model, facilitating projects (i.e. problems and change) within their team. Further development is required.
7.	Improved customer service quality and productivity associated with letter deliveries in metropolitan Delivery Centres.	Customer service performance nationally has improved to the highest level during the December 2002 quarter. South Australia has the best service standards of all mainland states. Customer complaints have declined 20-30% during the program. Not all success can be attributed to the Leadership Development program.
8.	An increased understanding of organisational learning and the benefits of developing a learning organisation culture in Australia Post.	Several participants have expressed a desire to continue with their learning. Change that has occurred to date is certainly a step in the right direction.
9.	Implementation of a continuous learning culture throughout all business units in South Australia and the Northern Territory.	The Adelaide Mail Centre leadership team has undertaken a program similar to that of the Delivery Business Unit. The Northern Territory has also embraced the concept of Action Learning, along with similar structure and process operating in their Delivery Centres.

SUMMARY

This case study describes the implementation of a work-applied leadership development program using the ARAL method for Australia Post's Delivery Business Unit of South Australia.

While it is recognised that the ARAL approach is not the only way of developing and implementing a learning and change program, the SMD has experienced encouraging outcomes from the project implemented at his workplace. The participants on the program had also learned and applied their knowledge to their Work-Based Projects.

This case study documents the results that can be achieved through applying the ARAL approach and this approach is recommended for implementing major change and learning and development programs in organisations.

REFERENCES

Abraham, S, Arnold, G & Oxenberry, R 1996, *The Self-Discovering Organisation: Fusing Action Research to the Learning Organisation*, presented at the conference on "Developing a Learning Organisation through Action Learning and Action Research", 25 & 26 Oct, organised by Action Learning, Action Research & Process Management Association Inc. & Singapore Institute of Management, in Singapore.

Abraham, S 1994, *Board management training for Indigenous community leaders using action research: the Kuju CDEP experience*. Port Lincoln Kuju CDEP Inc., Port Lincoln, SA.

Abraham, S 1997, *Exploratory Action Research for Manager Development*, Action Learning, Action Research & Process Management Association (ALARPM) Inc. and Gibaran Action Research Management Institute Pty Ltd, Queensland.

Cunningham, JB 1993, Action Research and *Organisational Development*, Praeger, Westport.

Kemmis, S & McTaggart, R 1988, *The Action Research Planner*, 3rd edition, Deakin University, Victoria.

McNiff, J 1992, *Action Research Principles and Practice*, Routledge, London.

Weinstein, K 1995 *Action Learning (A Journey in Discovery and Development)*, HarperCollins, Glasgow.

CHAPTER 3

MANAGEMENT LEARNING AND CHANGE
A WORK-APPLIED LEARNING APPROACH
Mohamad Bin Hashim

ABSTRACT

This chapter reports on a Work-Applied Learning (WAL) program using the Action Research and Action Learning (ARAL) approach which was developed and implemented for the senior management team of the Global Carriers Group which comprised Global Carriers Berhad, a public listed organisation in Malaysia, and its subsidiary companies.

This case study illustrates how the senior management team learnt the ARAL approach and applied it to manage the impact of the Asian financial crisis on the Global Carriers Group.

BACKGROUND

Global Carriers Berhad is a listed organisation on the Kuala Lumpur Stock Exchange and at the time of the project was the holding organisation of 21 subsidiary companies. All of these subsidiaries were involved in ship-owning and in shipping activities such as freight services, shipping management and ship agency services.

I founded the Global Carriers Group and was the Chief Executive Officer (CEO). I have extensive experience in services related to the oil and shipping industries, acquired over a period of 15 years with Shell Malaysia.

While the Global Carriers Group was growing rapidly, there was a concern amongst the Board members and myself that the management skills of the senior managers were not adequate for the changing nature of the Group, especially in view of its accelerated growth after listing. The specific concerns were as follows:

- There was a lack of integration as the senior managers did not work together for the benefit of the Global Carriers Group. Although

I encouraged teamwork and integration, I was unable to ensure that these practices were implemented because of the demands on my time to manage the growth of the Global Carriers Group.

- There were no departmental plans and the departments did not know how to work in teams to develop such plans. I did not have enough time to coach them.
- While the Global Carriers Group operated as effectively as it could, it was not operating at optimum efficiency and effectiveness.
- The pace of growth of the Global Carriers Group required a dynamic structure. However, it had been operating with an out-dated organisational structure which did not reflect its current services and manpower changes. As a result, there was a lack of role clarity, poor communications and regular conflict.
- Although the Global Carriers Group had grown at a rapid pace, there was a concern that there had not been a parallel growth in the competencies of the managers and in their ability to cope with the changes.

The Board of Directors and I realised that there was an urgent need for the senior managers to learn how to work together in teams and how to cope with and manage the changes which had resulted from the rapid growth of the Global Carriers Group.

As I was familiar with the concepts of ARAL, I convinced the Board of Directors that it was appropriate to introduce change in the Global Carriers Group through a WAL program using ARAL.

FORMING AN ACTION RESEARCH GROUP (AR GROUP)

I had a preliminary discussion with each senior manager about the concern shared by the Board of Directors of Global Carriers and myself that the managers did not have the management skills to cope with the changing nature of the Global Carriers Group and that we proposed implementing change through a WAL program using ARAL.

I then informed the senior managers that an Action Research Group (AR Group) would be set up to work through the change process and invited each of them to become members of this Group. I advised them that I was still in the process of learning more about the change process and would share further information with the AR Group in due course. I also emphasised that this process would help in their professional development as managers as well as the development of their respective departments.

In addition to the senior managers, I also invited the Special Projects Manager and the Project Consultant to join the AR Group. Each of the persons I invited agreed to join.

The AR Group therefore comprised:

- Commercial Manager
- Two Assistant Commercial Managers
- Crew Manager
- Assistant Crew Manager
- Operations Manager
- Assistant Operations Manager
- Finance Manager
- Human Resource Administrator
- Special Projects Manager
- Project Consultant

I invited Dr Selva Abraham, an expert on WAL, to talk to the AR Group about a WAL program using ARAL and its benefits for managers and organisations. After Dr Abraham spoke on the process and its benefits, all members of the AR Group gave their total support to the WAL program because they realised the benefits that could be derived from such a program.

Subsequent to this, I attended a five-day workshop facilitated by Dr Abraham at the Gibaran Management Institute in Adelaide. On my return to Malaysia, I told the AR Group about the benefits of WAL that I had learnt in Adelaide and suggested that Dr Abraham be invited to be a Resource Person for the AR Group. The AR Group agreed to this suggestion.

The following section describes the ARAL cycles that emerged in the WAL program.

THE ARAL CYCLES OF WAL

There were two major cycles in the WAL program.

Cycle 1
Cycle 1 was for a period of about nine months between May 1996 and January 1997 and comprised four mini-cycles. Lasting for about three to four months, each mini-cycle commenced with a Knowledge & Planning Workshop followed by a Work-Based Phase and AR Group meetings for observation and reflection.

At the end of the fourth mini-cycle, there was also an evaluation session and this marked the completion of Cycle 1.

The ARAL model for the WAL program that emerged in Cycle 1 is illustrated in Figure 3.1. As can be seen from the figure, the AR Group worked with the staff members of the Action Learning (AL) sets in each department and myself.

While the AR Group Members worked as a group for the introduction of the change process using AR, they also worked with their respective AL sets to introduce change in their departments. The integrated WAL approach, grounded in ARAL, therefore impacted on the Global Carriers Group as a whole because of the changes within the various departments.

Figure 3.1 – ARAL Model in Cycle 1

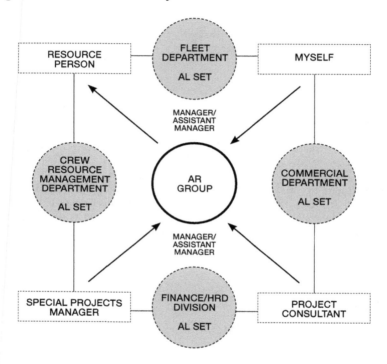

Mini Cycle 1.1
Knowledge Planning Workshop 1

I welcomed the AR Group Members and provided them with an update on the progress made by the Global Carriers Group over the last few years and the need to consolidate its operations through a change process. I then introduced Dr Selva Abraham, who would be a Resource Person during this change process.

The AR Group Members then discussed an issue related to human resource management. I indicated that the Global Carriers Group did not currently have a Human Resource Department. However, I expressed the hope that one of the outcomes of this program would be a recommendation by the AR Group Members for the establishment of such a department.

It was generally agreed that the Global Carriers Group was growing very rapidly, which may have resulted in this department not previously being set up. The AR Group Members agreed that there was a critical need for "consolidation" and "integration" before the Global Carriers Group entered the next phase of development.

Discussion continued on other problems related to strategic planning as perceived by the AR Group Members. It was suggested that strategic planning be done properly from now onward using a participative management style, and it was agreed that a committee should be formed to address this issue.

The Resource Person and I also discussed with the AR Group Members the principles and practice of Action Learning (AL) and the relationship between AL and Action Research (AR). The Resource Person explained in detail the model of the integrated ARAL approach, which works around the word formula AR=AL+C+R, and its relationships to Work-Applied Learning.

The AR Group Members then spent time developing "AL Project Briefs". I suggested that the projects to be undertaken by each of the AR Group Members should be based on the critical issues in their respective departments so that full benefit could be derived from such projects. I stressed that the projects should be real, meaningful and approved initially by the AR Group Members so that they could be integrated with each other.

Further discussions amongst the AR Group Members revolved around the issues of "What business are we in?" and "Business Transformation". Some AR Group Members listed the principal activities of the Global Carriers Group whilst others set out its broad and specific objectives and goals.

With the assistance of the Resource Person, I categorised the AR Group Members' thoughts into objectives, goals, and strategies, and a summary was produced showing the "business" of the Global Carriers Group. The AR Group Members then listed the various objectives which Global should consider in order to perform its "business" effectively.

Based on these objectives, the AR Group Members then proposed a suitable corporate structure for the Global Carriers Group so that it could fully perform its functions effectively and efficiently.

At the end of the Knowledge Planning Workshop, it was agreed that AR Group Members would form AL Sets in their departments, comprised of selected staff members. Each of these AL Sets would develop a purpose statement and short-term and long-term objectives for their respective departments, and work as a team to introduce whatever actions and changes they felt were appropriate.

Discussion continued on the structure and roles of the Group, and the rest of the time was used by the AR Group Members to start developing purpose statements for their own departments and discussing these with other members of the AR Group

It was agreed that the next Knowledge Planning Workshop, scheduled for July 1996, would be used to address the purposes, objectives and tactics for each department and that the AR Group Members should reflect on the current status of their departments by carrying out a "SWOT" (Strengths, Weaknesses, Opportunities, Threats) analysis, prior to establishing the objectives and tactics.

Mini Cycle 1.2
Knowledge & Planning Workshop 2

The AR Group Members discussed what their AL Sets had achieved during Mini Cycle 1 and the projects which were to be undertaken by each department. The objective of the discussion was two-fold: firstly, to get the Group to interact more with each other and secondly, to obtain feedback from other AR Group Members on the direction and objective of the proposed projects since such projects were to be linked to other departments.

Presentations were made by the AR Group Members on the status of the plans they had drawn up and the actions that their respective AL Sets had taken during Mini Cycle 1. The Resource Person and I were very satisfied and impressed with the fact that all the AR Group Members had delivered the outcomes as agreed.

After the presentations, the AR Group Members were introduced to the "Strategic Management Process" by the Resource Person and me. They noted that the Global Carriers Group had the following weaknesses: there was too much of an operational focus; it was crisis driven; there was a lack of managerial development; and there was a lack of integration between departments. Nevertheless, they also noticed certain strengths within the Group, namely that it had a sense of purpose, the staff members were committed and dedicated, and the Global Carriers Group was technically sound in shipping.

The AR Group Members spent the rest of the workshop identifying the strengths and weaknesses of their respective departments in order to help them determine relevant projects that could be initiated. They also discussed the process of Action Learning and reflected on how it could operate in their departments. The main points emerging from this discussion were:

- The AR Group Members were to give priority to the current critical issues of their respective departments. Action Learning processes should be developed to address these critical issues.

- With respect to the strategic plan, the AR Group Members agreed that the strategic plan for the entire Global Carriers Group should be developed progressively from "bottom-up".

  They felt that the ideas generated by their respective AL sets could be incorporated into the Global Carriers Group's vision and mission and the departmental goals. The final strategic plan would therefore be developed by the AR Group Members with the Special Projects Manager acting as facilitator.

The workshop ended on a positive note when I announced that I was pleased with the changes that were already evident as a result of the program and that I was confident more positive changes would take place during this Mini Cycle.

Mini Cycle 1.3
Knowledge Planning Workshop 3

After a brief reflection on what had been done so far in terms of Knowledge Workshops 1 and 2, I invited presentations from the AR Group Members on the actions taken during Mini Cycle 1.2 by the AL Sets of their respective departments. The following were the outcomes:

Administration/Human Resource Department (HRM)
The Human Resource Administrator presented the following report for the HRM AL Set:

First Six Month Plan (July to December 1996)
Human Resource

- to get the Board of Directors' approval on the proposed Terms and Conditions of Employment and the proposed grouping and salary structure;
- to draw up the current Organisational Structure of the Global Carriers Group and to define the function of each job clearly by compiling its job description and job specification.
- to develop a performance and yearly appraisal system and to implement the system (or at least part of it) for 1996 salary revision; and
- To formulate policy and guidelines for selection and recruitment.

Public Relations
- to organise a family day in 1996; and
- to gain a better understanding of the role of Public Relations.

Second Six Month Plan (January to July 1997)
Human Resource

- to formulate the Group's policy on discipline; and
- to improve on the administration of the Human Resource functions, i.e. annual leave procedures etc.

Public Relations

- to initiate contact with media; and
- to start co-ordinating information for an in-house newsletter.

The HRM Learning Set did not present its budget as a new Head of Department had been appointed recently and he wanted to familiarise himself with the Department before presenting the budget.

Finance Department (Finance)

The Finance Manager reminded the AR Group of the "Purpose, Short-Term and Long-Term Objectives" of Finance which had been presented during Knowledge Workshop 2 and advised that the Finance AL set wished to undertake the following projects:

- set up an Information Technology Department to oversee the computerisation of the entire office. This would ensure that all information would be up-to-date and readily available for operational and management purposes;
- set up an Internal Audit Department which would report directly to the Board of Directors. The Internal Audit Department would also have to assist the Fleet Department on the International Safety Management (ISM) Certification exercise;
- prepare a Manual of Authority on Group Procedures; and
- prepare an Annual Budget for the entire Group.

It was suggested that the Manual of Authority would set out guidelines on the amounts which are within the delegated authority of each level of management so that the CEO would not need to be involved in all financial transactions.

The Finance Manager reported that some departments had not yet presented their departmental budgets for consolidation into the company's Annual Budget. The AR Group Members were asked to submit their budgets as soon as possible as it would enable the senior management to monitor the progress of the Group.

Research/Strategic Issues Department (RSI)

The Special Projects Manager, who was in charge of the Research/Strategic Issues (RSI) Department, advised that the RSI AL Set would undertake the development of a strategic plan for the entire Global Carriers Group over a six month period, based on the input received from all departments. Upon receipt of input and after discussions with the relevant departments, the AL Set would undertake the task of analysing, cross validating and consolidating such input to formulate a strategic plan.

He also advised that management had decided on a further capital raising exercise and that two merchant banks had been shortlisted to present their proposals. Upon completion of the exercise, Global Carriers would be financially sound and would be established as a significant player in the shipping industry.

Crew Resource Management Department (CRM)

The Assistant Crew Manager reflected on the short-term and long-term plans which had been presented in Knowledge & Planning Workshop 2 and reported that the CRM Learning Set had undertaken the following:
- a review of the existing manning agents' contracts and the appointment of the Philippines' recruitment agency;
- continual review of the appointment and quality of existing masters and chief engineers in view of the rapid expansion of the Group's fleet of vessels;
- finalisation of its budget for submission to the Finance Department;
- an up-grade of the facilities on board certain vessels, especially the living accommodation; and
- completion of a comprehensive project on the salary structure of the shipping industry.

Commercial/Marketing Department (Commercial)

The Commercial Manager advised that the Commercial Learning Set had raised the following issues:
- the department's structure had to be finalised;
- the importance of marketing and the need for Commercial to work closely with Fleet and CRM; and
- although the Global Carriers Group had recently committed to purchasing four more vessels, additional funds had to be sourced to acquire more vessels.

He then presented the Commercial budget. I challenged the budget, suggesting that it was unrealistic and should be based on optimal circumstances rather than on past trends only.

Fleet Management Department (Fleet)

The Assistant Operations Manager presented the Fleet AL Set's action report and its project plans, which essentially revolved around the International Safety Management (ISM) certification. He raised the Fleet

AL Set's concerns about staff shortage in Fleet. It was agreed that this issue would have to be worked out with CRM as soon as possible.

This was followed by the presentation of the budget for the Fleet, based on the "best case" scenario, where all vessels were properly maintained with minimal breakdown time.

The Fleet was facing difficulty in coping with the current workload, which was largely attributable to the doubling in fleet size and the current implementation of the ISM Code.

Nevertheless, it was agreed by the AR Group Members that Fleet should review its current operations and increase its level of effectiveness and efficiency in order to move forward in line with the growth of the Group.

The final day of Knowledge & Planning Workshop 3 was devoted to providing the AR Group Members with further knowledge on strategic planning. In particular, the Resource Person and I introduced them to McKinsey's "7-S Framework" of introducing change.

Mini Cycle 1.4
Knowledge Workshop 4

I reflected with the AR Group members on the significant work that had been accomplished for the Group over the year with events such as:

- achieving public listing;
- investing more than RM$300 million in vessels after listing;
- increasing the number of vessels from 9 to 21; and
- more than doubling staff strength.

I pointed out that with such expansion new issues would arise and the Global Carriers Group will have to adjust in order to cope with various challenges. I added that this would result in, amongst other things, the setting up of formal procedures, policies and guidelines. I then urged the AR Group Members to work together to enable the Group to progress further in the coming year.

The major strategic plans for the following year were then presented to the Group, some of which were:

- investment of another RM$150 million;
- submission for a massive capital funding program; and
- the continuation of more investment in vessels.

The AR Group Members then reported on the status of actions and plans that had been proposed by their AL sets during Mini Cycle 1.3.

The Special Projects Manager presented two alternative re-structures for the merged Fleet and Commercial Departments:

- all seven functions under both Fleet and Commercial would report to one Head, who would in turn report to the Commercial Manager; or
- fleet and Commercial functions would be retained separately, whereby there would be two sub-section heads taking charge of the two functions. The two sub-section heads would report to the Head who would in turn report to the Commercial Manager.

Various issues were raised, such as the line of reporting for both the legal department and the audit department. The Resource Person and I urged the AR Group Members to discuss these issues further and refine the existing structure based on the various comments made by the AR Group. It was agreed by the AR Group Members that the Special Projects Manager would continue to work closely with the other departments in clarifying their roles and relationships and to recommend the most appropriate structure for the Group.

The Assistant Operations Manager also reported on the progress of the ISM implementation in the Fleet Department, which essentially revolved around safety and pollution control. Extensive work had been done on the ISM, given the extensive draft manuals that had been completed. According to the Assistant Operations Manager, the process was on schedule and would be completed by the mandatory deadline.

The other AR Group Members stated that their AL Sets were acting on the plans and that they would report on their progress at the next Knowledge & Planning Workshop.

I shared with the Group that I was pleased to have received feedback on many issues, successes and shortcomings which I would not have known about in normal circumstances. I was also pleased to note that the AR Group Members had all been open in the discussions as this would lead to closer integration and learning from each other. Nevertheless, I noted that there was still a communication gap between Fleet and Commercial which made the proposed merger of the two departments problematic. I stated that the ARAL approach would assist in this and lead to greater effectiveness and efficiency of the whole Group.

We continued with the concept of McKinsey's 7-S Framework, which had been started during Knowledge & Planning Workshop 3, and discussed in detail the type of Structure, Strategy, Systems, Style, Staff, and Skills which were required to achieve the Shared Vision of the Group. The AR Group and I agreed that this strategic change process would be reflected upon at the next Knowledge & Planning Workshop in the context of the long term plans of the Global Carriers Group.

The second day of the Knowledge & Planning Workshop was spent in reflecting and evaluating the impact of the ARAL approach and change process in the Global Carriers Group.

At the end of the Knowledge & Planning Workshop, the Resource Person advised the AR Group Members that he believed they were ready to continue the change process without him and that he would be available if they needed his expertise. He suggested that the AR Group should also seek other knowledge specialists to work with them, if and when necessary.

Final Evaluation/Validation Stage

The process of final evaluation and validation of Cycle 1 of the WAL program was as follows:

> **Step 1:**
> I provided a report on my observation of the mini-cycles of Cycle 1.

> **Step 2:**
> The AR Group Members were given half an hour to read my report and were invited to individually confirm whether the data recorded was accurate and complete, both with regard to the overall process and the changes that had been introduced in their respective departments. In addition, the Resource Person was also asked to comment on the report.

> **Step 3:**
> The AR Group Members were also invited to comment on their perceptions of the impact of the ARAL approach on their respective departments.

The AR Group Members confirmed that all my observations with regard to changes in their respective departments were accurate and the mini-cycle processes had been correctly reported.

They also reported that over the previous six months, they had moved from a situation of being crisis-driven and lacking in planning and organising to one where planning processes were in place and some of the plans had actually been introduced.

The perceptions of the AR Group Members of the impact that the ARAL approach had on their respective departments are as follows:

Fleet Department
The Assistant Operations Manager's comments on changes in the Fleet Department as a result of the WAL were as follows:

> The ARAL process had already brought about positive changes to the whole Group. It was delegated from the top, in particular by the CEO himself. Constant monitoring and evaluation are being carried out. Within the Fleet Department, we are producing regular reports such as:
>
> - monthly Operating Expenses Reports — these are evaluated against the budgeted expenses and unbudgeted expenses need to be justified;
>
> - monthly down-time reports to reflect on a vessel's performance, thus checking on how well the maintenance has been carried out;
>
> - quarterly crew evaluation reports to reflect on crew's performance; priority was given to assessment of senior officers on board as that determined the control of shipboard operations and crew productivity; and
>
> - regular inspection reports by the Superintendent after each ship visit.

From the vessels, regular reporting and feedback on operations and maintenance is currently being done as the Safety Management System of the ISM code is being initiated. The views of the Operations Manager on the impact of the ARAL approach on the Fleet Department were as follows:

> ARAL did help improve my competencies in management and planning change in my department.
>
> I have led my team in the implementation of change by introducing management controls. I delegate to enable the achievement of the best possible results from each delegation. I have learnt what is prioritising; how to delegate; how to choose the right person for the job; how to recognise and overcome barriers and manage crisis.
>
> Over the last six months, the staff has become more motivated, loyal, confident and they have learnt to overcome the Malaysian cultural barrier of the staff–management relationship to give feedback to management.

Commercial Department

The Assistant Commercial Manager commented that the following changes had resulted from the ARAL approach:

> The operations functions of the Commercial Department have been transferred to the Fleet Department. Account Executives have been developed through the Action Learning process to handle operational aspects of commercial shipping such as monitoring freight payments, analysing claims, issuing bills, invoices and debit notes, direct communication with clients and follow-up on payments.
>
> These changes have moved the account executives from being clerks to accountable junior executives. The Manager and I are now able to concentrate on more strategic issues for the Department. However, we realise that we need more knowledge in negotiation skills and business development skills, as well as advanced courses in the ship chartering business.

The Commercial Manager reported:

> Over the last six months, the Commercial Department has gone through major changes. Some senior managers have resigned as they could not cope with those changes. However, by working closely together, the Assistant Commercial Manager and I have created a learning environment and the enthusiastic and innovative staff who have suitable experience have moved up in the department over the last few months.
>
> The Department is now more able to cope with crisis and strategic changes. The Action Learning process has definitely contributed to these changes.

Finance and Research and Strategic Issues Departments

The Special Projects Manager commented that exposure to the ARAL approach had a major bearing on his performance and the performance of his departments, which were restructured to include the Finance Department following the resignation of the Finance Manager. He described the impact on each department as follows:

> When I took over the Finance Department from the Finance Manager, I was new to the department in the sense of how the department was run. I found a little difficulty in settling down initially. In this respect I changed first before I introduced change into the department. I changed my mode of thinking completely, and settled down so that I could fit into the way the department was run.

After that I created a learning environment for the staff to be more innovative, independent and adaptable.

I held regular meetings, in fact daily meetings, with my staff on how to handle the creditors e.g. who to pay and who not to pay first etc. Basically this is to give an indication of how the team should be heading. I believe this provides some kind of direction to the staff through my leadership.

Now things are getting better, I still request my staff to continue monitoring the creditors but without the necessity of holding the daily meetings. The staff can now handle problems on their own and occasionally they will give me their feedback.

Now my role is to make sure that the suppliers and customers are happy i.e. my staff have to be more externally orientated rather than internally oriented.

Some of the achievements of the previous Finance Manager and his AL Set were:

- monthly management information is now readily available;
- the budget has been completed as a result of the improved commitment and teamwork; and
- initiation of the process of re-alignment of traditional departmental functions and role clarity emerging.

Gaps identified in Finance by the previous Finance Manager were:

- the need for processes to provide adequate time for payment of vessels; and
- the need for further clarification of roles.

Research and Strategic Issues Department
The Special Projects Manager stated:

I continue to oversee this function and I am responsible to the CEO for coordinating the research and strategic issues of the Group. We have come a long way in the development of a strategy document from six months ago when all strategy was only in the mind of the CEO.

As a coordinator, I feel that the departmental managers are beginning to think and talk strategically and I am confident that within the next six months major changes will take place in the Group.

Human Resource Management (HRM) Department

The Human Resource Manager/Company Secretary stated that the ARAL process had definitely resulted in the initiation of change in the HRM department. His comments were as follows:

> Strategic planning has been initiated in the HRM Department using the Action Learning process. The AL Set is made up of staff members who are motivated and enthusiastic because they are able to share their ideas and contribute to the development of the department.
>
> An ARAL project that has been initiated is the salary structure for staff. Information is currently being gathered from other shipping companies on salaries and other benefits.
>
> Another Action Learning project that is ongoing is the development of middle managers. Set members are currently gathering information from directors and senior managers on what middle management competencies are required by the Group.
>
> With respect to the re-organisation, some of the key issues raised are set out below:
> * centralisation vs. decentralisation;
> * authority vs. power;
> * delegation vs. abdication;
> * responsibility; and
> * staff authority.

Crew Resource Management (CRM) Department

The Crew Manager had the following comments on the ARAL approach:

> CRM has initiated new and additional training programs for crew members. We are introducing a form of AL process in this training so that the crew members can work more effectively as a team on board the ships.
>
> We have also initiated hospital and insurance benefit schemes over the last six months. New compensation schemes in relation to productivity and performance have been introduced. We have also received many staff suggestions in relation to productivity and will review them.
>
> During the next six months the Human Resource Department and the Crew Resource Management Department will be integrated and that will increase the efficiency of the Group.

Observations of the Resource Person:

> After the first Knowledge & Planning Workshop, I was amazed to note that a Group of this size had no plans and no strategies; the sole focus of the Group was on its shipping operations.
>
> What I have seen over the last six months is the positive impact of the ARAL approach in changing individual and departmental behaviour.

Reflections on Cycle 1

The WAL process is represented in Figure 3.2 and the results for the senior managers of the shipping company were as follows:

1. Senior managers in the past had no plans for their departments. However, after the ARAL approach was introduced, the Action Learning (AL) sets within the Fleet Department, the Crew Resource Management Department, the Human Resource Department, and the Finance Department each developed departmental plans.
2. The observations of the AR Group Members, the Resource Person and myself all confirmed the initiatives that were involved in the implementation of the plan by each department through the AL Sets.
3. The Human Resources Department and the Research and Strategic Issues Department were established to cope with the needs of a growing Group.
4. The AR Group Members worked together as an integrated team and this was not evident before Cycle 1.

Prior to the introduction of change, there was no integration between the departmental senior managers. However, the WAL program not only brought the departmental managers together but also the departmental managers worked more closely with their department staff through the AL Sets.

Figure 3.2 – Cycle 1 WAL Process using ARAL

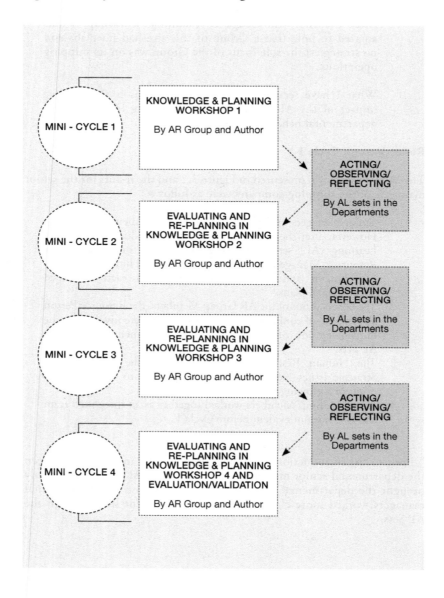

Cycle 2

Whilst Cycle 1 took six months to complete, Cycle 2 covered a period of two and a half years. During the first mini cycle, it was decided that the future cycles should focus on the Asian financial crisis and on managing its impact on the Group.

In addition to this, working together with the AR Group, the current AL sets in their respective departments would continue working on implementing their departmental plans. The Planning/Action/Observation stages of the three mini-cycles in Cycle 2 are presented below, followed by a description of the Reflection/Evaluation stage:

Mini-Cycle 2.1
Knowledge Planning Workshop 5

I welcomed the AR Group Members and briefed them on the developments which had occurred since the end of Cycle 1.

I distributed the notes of the previous Knowledge & Planning Workshop to the AR Group Members, after which I spoke about the importance of having a "Shared Vision", one of the 7-S of the "McKinsey 7S Framework" of introducing change.

The session continued with a video presentation on "Vision" by Joel Baker, followed by a group discussion on the video. I distributed to each departmental head their respective documents on vision/objectives/plans which had been developed during Cycle 1.

Time was given for the AR Group members to reflect on these documents, after which I requested feedback on whether the present organisational structure would continue to be effective in the light of its present and future developments such as:

- the Global Carriers Group had increased its fleet size from 9 vessels to 21 vessels in a period of just over 12 months; and
- the company was in the process of raising RM$500 million from the capital market to purchase more vessels.

I suggested that the AR Group should undertake a strategic review of the Global Carriers Group and its departments for the next three years and then on an annual basis. This would ensure a regular assessment of the effectiveness of the Global Carriers Group and its structure.

The Knowledge & Planning Workshop continued with action report presentations from the departments, which are summarised below:

Fleet Department

The Assistant Operations Manager reported on the Fleet Department's on-going implementation of the ISM Code, with its focus on maritime safety and pollution. I was pleased to note that implementation of the ISM Code was on target for completion by the mandatory deadline. The Assistant Operations Manager confirmed that the implementation process had been properly minuted and copies of the minutes had been regularly submitted to management.

The Finance/Strategic Issues Manager (formerly the Special Projects Manager) voiced his concern that the ISM Manual would become another "white elephant". The Assistant Operations Manager assured the AR Group Members that the ISM Manual would be very useful in preparing the Global Carriers Group for audits by the Malaysian Marine Department. The audits would be carried out annually on office procedures and every two and a half years for procedures on board vessels; and the Global Carriers Group could be reprimanded for non-compliance.

Human Resource Department (HRM)

The Human Resource Manager/Company Secretary presented a list of the purpose/objectives/areas of concern for HRM which had been initiated and documented by the previous head of department.

I noted that although some policies had been implemented, they had not been properly documented whilst others had been documented (in full or in part) but not implemented. The Human Resource Manager/Company Secretary undertook to collate those policies which had been documented and implemented.

Finance Department

The Finance/Strategic Issues Manager reflected on the objectives (short/long term) of the Finance Department, established during the previous Mini-cycles. One of the objectives was the completion of the annual audit which was the toughest because it was the first audit since Global Carriers was listed on the Kuala Lumpur Stock Exchange. I was pleased to note that the preliminary audit had been completed on time, before the mandatory deadline.

The Finance/Strategic Issues Manager then touched on the progress of each of the short-term objectives set earlier for the Finance Department. He also raised the issues of the late remittance of crew salaries and home allotments which had not been resolved. After a lively discussion among the AR Group Members on these issues and how they could be resolved, they concluded that these problems arose mainly due to the lack of preparation and follow-up action by the Group.

Due to the shortage of time, it was decided that Crew Resource Management and Finance would form an AL Set to establish the procedures for handling these issues.

I noted that the above presentations had identified several critical issues for which procedures and policies needed to be established. After some discussion, it was agreed that the format and presentation of the procedures and policies should be done by the respective departments in a simple yet comprehensive format.

Crew Resource Management
The Assistant Crew Manager reported that one of the major action plans implemented by his department was the formulation of the Terms and Conditions of Employment, which had been distributed to the various Heads of Department.

Commercial
The Assistant Commercial Manager reminded the AR Group Members that as the Commercial Department was the marketing department in the Group, its main responsibility was to generate optimum revenue from the efficient carriage of goods by vessels through offering reliable schedules and customer-oriented service.

He then set out the short- and long-term objectives of the department, which had been established during the previous Knowledge & Planning Workshops, and provided brief explanations for each. He also provided flowcharts for procedures such as Chartering Procedures and Post-Fixtures and Operations Procedures. It was noted that most of the short- and long-term objectives of the department, which were either in the implementation stage or had been completed, were essentially internal procedures.

The objectives which had not been achieved were more 'external' in nature and related to the development of new markets and new products, such as the identification of carriage of palm oil and the establishment of services to other routes.

Strategic Research/Finance Issues
The Finance/Strategic Issues Manager briefly explained that the Strategic/Research Issues Department was essentially responsible for the strategic development of the Group. After setting out the short- and long-term objectives of the department, he then explained which of those had been achieved and which were being implemented.

The Finance/Strategic Issues Manager mentioned that the role of his department was long-term in nature and, as such, the results would not be obvious for some time. Brief mention was made of the RM$500 million capital-raising exercise and how it would impact on the Group. Planning for this capital-raising exercise was expected to be completed about one and a half years after commencement.

Using McKinsey's 7-S Framework of introducing change, the Finance/Strategic Issues Manager explained how his department would work with the other departments of the Global Carriers Group to achieve the Shared Vision.

The Finance/Strategic Issues Manager then raised the following issues:

- each department was looking at their own interests rather than looking at it from the Group's point of view;
- lack of communication between departments compounded the issues; and
- some employees had a 'hands-off' attitude towards some operational problems and matters not specifically related to them. Rather than assisting during critical times, they had a tendency to 'pass the buck' to other departments.

I then observed that great progress had been made by the respective departments based on the achievement of established objectives and added that procedures and policies arising from such progress should be properly formalised in order to provide direction for others to follow.

I urged the AR Group to continue to improve communications and integration as this had been an ongoing issue since the beginning of the WAL program. Whatever the shortcomings and problems, each department should also not stop innovating and improving their performance.

In my closing remarks, I noted with pleasure that the changes, the ensuing discussions and the results achieved were new experiences for Global Carriers. I was also pleased that there was a 'positive intention and sincerity' during the discussions to address the various critical issues and problems. The presentations had also created a better understanding of the functions of the other departments and this was expected to establish better co-operation and integration amongst departments.

I requested the AR Group to take note of the following:

- each department had to submit updates of action plans;
- completed plans were to be formalised and submitted for compilation;
- work-in-progress should be prioritised and followed up by the Finance/Strategic Issues Manager; and
- uncompleted action plans were to be followed up closely.

The AR Group continued with the regular operational meetings as they became a useful forum for discussing issues of concern with the various departments, such as the need for implementing new policies or deciding on corporate restructuring.

One of the results of the regular AR Group meetings was that the various departments began working more closely to resolve problematic situations.

The AR Group decided that a Systems Development Policy should be adopted immediately, so that all activities were aligned and procedures could be implemented for checking and counter-checking activities and processes. It was agreed that each department would be required to submit a list of its procedures and activities to the Systems Coordinator. After having detailed discussions with each department on its procedures and activities, the Systems Coordinator would then draft a set of procedures for comment, amendment, eventual approval and adoption.

Other strategic changes that were discussed and agreed upon were as follows:

- the Commercial, Fleet and Crew Resource Management divisions would be sub-divided into Liquid, Dry Bulk and Containers sections;
- operations Department would be transferred from Commercial to Fleet;
- commercial would concentrate on fixing cargo and liaising with the charterers;
- CRM would handle the recruitment and arrangements for the boarding of new crew and repatriation of crew signing off;
- all communications with vessels and the management of crew on board would be the responsibility of the Operations Department. However, where the Operations Department recommends a change of crew, in the case of problems, CRM would be responsible for repatriation of that crew and the recruitment and boarding of a replacement crew;
- the heads of the Crew Resource Management Department and the Fleet Department would report to the Manager, Commercial Division, who in turn would report to the CEO; and
- a new department would be set up within the Fleet Division to monitor the construction of vessels commissioned by the Global Carriers Group.

Mini-Cycle 2.2
The Malaysian Government had a policy of aggressively promoting the development of Malaysian ports, shipping and its related industries.

In April 1997, as a result of the conducive economic environment and the encouraging prospects of the shipping industry, the Global Carriers Group had committed to the construction of six new products and chemical tankers costing a total of approximately RM$280 million.

Global Carriers proposed to finance the construction of these tankers and the acquisition of other vessels through a Rights Issue of RM$500 million. The balance of the proceeds of the Rights Issue exercise would be used to repay at least 80% of Global Carriers' borrowings. Arab–Malaysian Merchant Bank Berhad (AMMB) was appointed as Global Carriers' advisor, Managing Underwriter and Lead Manager of the Rights Issue.

The Rights Issue was subsequently approved by the Securities Commission for the revised sum of RM$400 million (instead of the RM$500 million originally proposed). The shareholders of Global Carriers approved the Rights Issue for completion.

However, the unexpected Asian economic crisis was a shock and a major change in the external environment. The Thai economy crashed as confidence in its financial markets deteriorated. This situation had an inevitable ripple effect on the Malaysian economy and in the wider Asian region. The Malaysian Ringgit fell to new lows against the US Dollar. The stock markets continued to fall as foreign investors became increasingly nervous because of the uncertainty in the Asian markets and withdrew their investment funds from the Kuala Lumpur Stock Exchange.

The Malaysian Finance Minister in his budget speech announced belt-tightening measures, which effectively led to bank financing being difficult to obtain and working capital facilities being withdrawn from companies.

The economic crisis had major implications for the Global Carriers Group, the most serious of which were as follows:

- cancellation of the Rights Issue;
- withdrawal of working capital facilities;
- higher interest charges;
- reduced confidence by foreign suppliers;
- increased foreign debts;
- delay in freight receipts and
- depressed freight rates.

Three additional AL sets, namely, the Finance, Restructuring and Operations AL sets, attempted to cope with the impact of the Asian financial crisis on the Global Carriers Group, whilst the AL sets established in Cycle 1 continued to operate the business. The ARAL model that emerged in Cycle 2 is provided in Figure 3.3.

Figure 3.3 – ARAL Model in Cycle 2

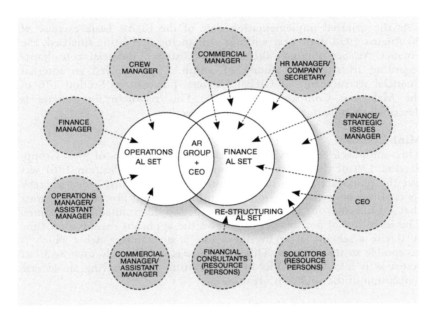

In this turbulent environment of the Asian economic crisis, the AR Group changed its emphasis from the departments to the Global Carriers Group as a whole by dividing themselves into the Finance AL Set, the Re-structuring AL Set and the Operations Learning Set and then used an integrated ARAL approach to its maximum.

Finance AL Set
When the full impact of the economic crisis was becoming obvious to the Global Carriers Group, the AR Group Members and I decided to establish a Finance AL Set comprising certain members of the AR Group, to manage the corporate finance functions. It would also manage the implementation of the Rights Issue.

The Finance AL Set consisted of four persons, namely:

- Commercial Manager;
- Finance/Strategic Issues Manager;
- Company Secretary/Human Resource Manager; and
- myself as CEO.

The Finance AL Set was kept small because of the confidential nature of its duties. Its main focus was to locate financiers, either local or international, institutional bankers or private investors who would finance the Rights Issue exercise or provide some sort of financing amounting to RM$400 million.

The Finance AL Set met almost every working day to review and assess the status of the various financing deals that the set was negotiating.

As the deferred implementation date of the Rights Issue exercise of 30 August 1998 drew near without a financing deal being finalised, the Finance AL Set obtained the advice of external financial consultants regarding an alternative course of action. This involved an internal financial restructuring of Global Carriers, pursuant to Section 176 of the Malaysian Companies Act 1965. This restructuring exercise is described in more detail in the following section.

Mini-Cycle 2.3
This mini-cycle dealt with the re-structuring phase of the Group. Section 176 of the Malaysian Companies Act 1965 (Section 176) sets out the procedure for an organisation to obtain a court order whereby its creditors are restrained from instituting any legal proceedings against that organisation for the duration of a period determined by the court. The intention of Section 176 is to give the applicant organisation time to devise a scheme of arrangement for its outstanding debts which is acceptable to its creditors. This procedure is usually only used as a last resort as it invariably results in the investing public having an adverse perception of the applicant organisation.

A Restructuring AL Set was formed to consider the option of the Section 176 procedure in greater detail. This set consisted of the existing Finance AL Set namely:

- Commercial Manager;
- Finance/Strategic Issues Manager; and
- Company Secretary/Human Resource Manager; and
- myself and 5 external consultants as follows:
  - 3 external financial consultants; and
  - 2 external solicitors.

The external facilitative consultants and solicitors were included in the restructuring AL Set as they could provide expert advice as resource people as well as access to their network of contacts in financial circles. The Restructuring AL Set also sought legal advice on a regular basis in order that the set could learn about the major risks of a Section 176 procedure.

The Restructuring AL Set learnt that the Section 176 procedure protected the applicant organisation only from legal proceedings instituted in Malaysia. Global Carriers was therefore not protected against any legal action which was initiated overseas.

Being shipping organisations, the Global Carriers Group was very vulnerable as its vessels plied international waters and more than 90% of its trade creditors (creditors who had supplied goods or services) were based overseas.

If these foreign trade creditors were unpaid for any length of time in respect of goods or services that they had supplied to any vessel, they could quite easily obtain a court order from the admiralty court in their country to enable them to arrest that vessel. The vessel would usually be impounded until some form of settlement was reached, usually payment in full.

It was therefore imperative that the foreign trade creditors should be handled very carefully so that they would not take any legal action against Global Carriers by arresting any of its vessels.

After careful planning, the entire senior management staff were mobilised to make contact with all trade creditors, both local and foreign, in order to explain Global Carriers' financial situation, and diffuse any possible legal action which these trade creditors might be considering. Letters were sent to all trade creditors to briefly explain the objectives and benefits of the proposed restructuring process that Global Carriers intended to implement. In addition, plans were put in place for the senior management staff to meet personally with the major foreign trade creditors within two weeks of the letters being sent, in order to explain the situation further.

The amount owed by Global Carriers to its financial creditors (creditors who were financial institutions), exceeded RM$500 million. Although this was a significant amount, the financial creditors were all Malaysian institutions and, as such, they would be bound by the Section 176 order when it was issued. They would therefore be unable to take any form of legal action against Global Carriers for the duration of the Section 176 order. In view of this, it was decided by the Restructuring AL Set that the financial creditors would be contacted after the Section 176 order was obtained.

The Section 176 order was granted for a period of 9 months. An announcement about this order was officially made to the Kuala Lumpur Stock Exchange, and was duly reported in the local newspapers.

As the trade creditors, both local and foreign, had previously been informed of this development, they did not react negatively to the announcement and the shipping operations carried on as usual. The financial creditors, on the other hand, were taken by surprise at the announcement, but being local institutions they were bound by the Section 176 order.

Having achieved protection against legal proceedings, the Restructuring AL Set then focussed on a restructuring scheme for Global Carriers. This scheme essentially involved a conversion of the existing debt into equity and cheaper forms of fixed coupon loan stocks, whereby Global Carriers' financial creditors would be given shares or loan stock in the organisation in exchange for the release of the debt. The result of this exercise would be to extinguish Global Carriers' debt, which was the same effect as the Rights Issue exercise which had been aborted earlier.

To ensure that the restructuring exercise was completed as soon as possible, it was necessary for appropriate Global Carriers staff to:

i) formulate schemes which would be acceptable to the financial creditors;

ii) negotiate with all the financial creditors in order to obtain feedback and, where possible, incorporate them into the relevant scheme; and

iii) co-ordinate the roles and responsibilities of the various professionals involved such as merchant bankers, accountants, share registers, etc.

For the financial institutions to agree to convert the existing debts owed to them by Global Carriers into equity and/or loan stocks in the organisation, Global Carriers had to be an attractive investment opportunity. Therefore, it was necessary for Global Carriers' shipping operations to be viable and profitable. To this end, an Operations AL Set was formed by the AR Group Members to review and improve the Group's shipping operations.

The Operations AL Set was made up of the following persons:

- Manager, Commercial Division;
- Assistant Commercial Manager;
- Crew Manager;
- Operations Manager;
- Assistant Operations Manager; and
- Company Secretary/HR Manager.

The Operations AL Set was requested by the AR Group Members and myself to undertake the following activities:

- undertake a SWOT (Strengths, Weaknesses, Opportunities and Threats) analysis of the Group;
- collect and collate certain data on the performance of each department;
- produce a set of key objectives which address, in quantitative terms, the desired targets and performance measures;
- establish plans and strategies to achieve the objectives;
- develop detailed programs and budgets for each of the departmental activities which contribute to the overall strategy; and
- monitor actual outputs against the targeted outputs.

The Operations AL Set identified the following problem areas:

- lack of cash resources to properly handle creditors and purchases;
- lack of cost control, mainly in purchasing;
- lack of a clearly established marketing plan;
- lack of a clear demarcation of the sales and responsibilities of the various departments;
- lack of business directions from the departmental directors;
- lack of planning for fleet maintenance;
- lack of urgency in responding to problems;
- lack of co-ordination both within departments and between departments;
- lack of motivation and team spirit amongst the staff; and
- the staff being reactive rather than proactive.

Some of the operational plans implemented by the Operations AL Set were as follows:

- optimal utilisation of vessels;
- the disposal or laying-up of uneconomic vessels;
- improved collection of freight;
- more efficient management of existing and potential creditors such as obtaining the largest credit period and getting goods and resources at the best prices possible; and
- better cost control measures and improvement in efficiency.

When the Operations AL Set meetings started in October 1998, they were lengthy, detailed and probing, as the focus was to identify and address potential problems before they got worse. The atmosphere at these meetings was cautious, defensive and resistant, as there were numerous problematic issues, mainly between the Fleet and Commercial Departments.

As the meetings of the Operations AL Set progressed over months, there was a gradual change in the prevailing atmosphere, as well as the attitude of the set members as follows:

- the set members became more open in raising issues to be resolved;
- there was greater interaction between the members in discussing and resolving issues;
- they were more results-oriented;
- there was an increased level of commitment to the Group; and
- the set members became more comfortable about challenging and questioning the assumptions of other set members in order to resolve issues of concern.

The meetings continued to be lengthy and intense as objectives which had not been met were continuously re-visited until they were achieved.

The difficulties faced by the set members in achieving the objectives were openly discussed and reviewed at these meetings.

Due to the improving interaction among the set members, an increasing number of options for overcoming such difficulties were usually canvassed, and acceptable courses of action were agreed upon.

The actions of the Operations Learning Set, coupled with the improving economic conditions in Malaysia resulted in the following positive outcomes:

- trade creditors no longer threatened legal action for failure to pay debts;
- trade creditors restored the original credit terms and no longer demanded cash on delivery;
- the vessels were operating at optimal levels, without any unplanned downtime, except for breakdowns in exceptional circumstances;
- freight collection was on time;
- the scheduled deadlines and costs for the mandatory day-docking of the vessels were properly monitored and adhered to;
- crew salaries were paid without any delay; and
- cost cutting measures, such as laying up of surplus vessels, changing to cheaper crews and purchasing controls, were gradually implemented without causing major disruption to current operations.

These positive results boosted the morale of the Operations AL Set members and gave them a sense of common direction and satisfaction which had not been obvious before the set was formed.

As time went on, the Operations AL Set was operating smoothly and effectively. The set members were responsible and accountable for the performance of their respective departments. Although there were still a few conflicts among set members, they were more focussed and willing to work towards the common goal of improving the shipping operations of the Group.

In the meantime, the restructuring exercise had progressed to the stage where Global Carriers had to obtain the in-principle approvals of the restructuring scheme from the financial creditors, before calling for a Creditors' Meeting to formally obtain their approval to the restructuring scheme.

The court-convened Creditors' Meeting was scheduled and Global Carriers was confident that, as a result of the improvement in both the internal shipping operations of the Global Carriers Group and the external economic conditions, a majority of the financial creditors would agree to the restructuring scheme which would eventually make them shareholders of the Group.

However, one financial creditor raised some technical issues in respect of the restructuring scheme. After lengthy discussions with the external consultants on the legal and financial implications of such an action, the Restructuring AL Set eventually decided to postpone the Creditors' Meeting.

The Creditors' Meeting was eventually held after the technical issues had been resolved. At this meeting, 60% of the creditors agreed to the restructuring scheme, and Global Carriers decided to adjourn the meeting for the other creditors. At the meeting, all but one of the creditors agreed to the scheme. This last creditor requested a further postponement. Numerous discussions were held with that creditor to consider the terms and conditions proposed by that creditor. Finally, that creditor advised Global Carriers of its approval of the scheme.

An Official Creditors' Meeting was finally held to enable this last creditor to formally approve the restructuring scheme.

Final Evaluation/Validation Stage
The processes of final evaluation and validation of Cycle 2 of the WAL approach using ARAL were as follows:

Step 1:
The CEO provided a report on his observation of the mini-cycles of Cycle 2 of the ARAL process (as set out in the preceding sections).

Step 2:
The AR Group Members were given thirty minutes to read the author's report and were invited to individually confirm whether the data recorded in the CEO's report was accurate and complete, both with regard to the overall process and the changes that had occurred in the Global Carriers Group. Half a day was used to reflect on the AR Group Members' responses.

Step 3:
An external validator conducted a semi-structured interview with the CEO and every AR Group Member to ascertain their individual perceptions of the impact of the WAL using an AR approach on the Global Carriers Group.

The information obtained from these data sources was triangulated so that there was an opportunity to compare and crosscheck the consistency of the findings on the impact that the ARAL approach had on the change process of the Global Carriers Group during Cycle 2. The AR Group Members all confirmed that the observations of the CEO with regard to changes in the Global Carriers Group were accurate and the mini-cycle processes had been correctly reported.

The perceptions of the AR Group Members of the impact that the ARAL approach had on the Global Carriers Group during Cycle 2 are set out below.

The Assistant Operations Manager's comments on changes in the Global Carriers Group as a result of the WAL program using the ARAL approach were as follows:

> The ARAL process has helped in the overall strategy of the Group. We have regular operational meetings, review our activities, have more discussions to help solve problems and develop policies as corrective action.

> AL has also helped us to cope with the economic crisis. The main thing we looked into was how to solve the financial problems. I was involved in talking to creditors and suppliers on a day-to-day basis and we used what we learnt from AL. We had a long list of creditors who all wanted to be paid. We had to negotiate with them and try to postpone payment if possible. That involved a lot of planning, acting on the plan and replanning so that we paid each one over a period of time. We kept the communication going not only within the Global Carriers Group but also with supplier-creditors rather than avoiding them because we had to regain their confidence.

The Operations Manager had the following comments:

> Through AL we are more organised. We identified our weaknesses and overcame our weaknesses by changing the strategies, the approach, the people.

> We have learnt to plan, act, observe and re-plan based on the outcome of our original plan.

> For example, the Fleet Department usually spent a lot of time on maintaining the old ships; however, they did not provide revenue for the Group. After many discussions, we decided to stop the operation of the old ships. We laid up those ships to minimise the maintenance cost and concentrated on the ships that generated revenue.

> We discussed with our team the department's structure. We realised that there was a lot of confusion and so we came up with another plan. Each ship manager had to be responsible for the ship he is assigned to, not like previously where the Head of Operations took charge of all the ships.

The Assistant Commercial Manager said:

> Before the ARAL process, we had casual meetings on an ad hoc basis, and did not keep any proper minutes. With AR we have well-prepared agenda points prepared from the Managers, and we have operational meetings which are very useful.

> Part of the benefits for us is that the CEO is also involved in chairing the operational meetings and if there are critical issues, he can make a decision without delay.

> With operational meetings things go on more smoothly and barriers have broken down. There are now direct lines of communication between middle management and top management.

> We have learnt important skills — to plan, execute, review and re-plan. This is a good tool but other tools are still lacking like marketing and communication skills.

> There is more delegation of authority and the staff get quality work satisfaction as they are directly involved in decision making. However, the lower level management staff need training in many areas.

The Commercial Manager commented as follows:

> My assistant, the Assistant Commercial Manager, and I feel that change in the department and in the Global Carriers Group has definitely occurred. AL has made us realise how important it is to monitor all our activities to check if we have to make changes to the way we do things.

> A lot of changes were planned for the Global Carriers Group like restructuring, expansion programs, market strategies, financing and organisation structure etc. but these were put on hold.

The Finance/Strategic Issues Manager had the following views on the impact that the ARAL process had on the Group:

> Before we introduced the ARAL process, there was no structured planning — most of our ideas or plans were on an ad-hoc basis and could happen any time during the day.

> When the Asian economic crisis struck, all our capital raising plans were put on hold. In fact, it was eventually aborted.

> We had to change our plan. Rather than thinking of moving

outwardly in expansion or acquisition of vessels, we started thinking inwardly in focusing on our Group. We started rationalising our operations, cutting down costs, focusing more on the existing fleet and optimising the revenue that we generate from the vessels. Basically, it was a consolidation process.

We were focusing more on controlling the cash flow rather than thinking about getting fresh capital to expand the business operations. This involved a lot of re-planning and realignment of staff, including realignment of my work to focus on different areas of activities and responsibilities.

In the early days, the CEO made all the decisions and everybody just followed whether the direction was right or wrong. With the introduction of the ARAL process, the CEO held regular meetings with the AR Group and everybody started to work as a team towards the agreed goal. AR has actually allowed the Group to work together and achieve what they set out to achieve.

The process of working together did not stop during the crisis and was, in fact, more vigorous and actually helped us to cope with the crisis.

The Human Resource Manager/Company Secretary's views were as follows:

The ARAL process has helped us to have better systems in place. When there is an issue, we take swift action, we look at various options before implementation and we consistently review our procedures. We are continually evaluating how to do things better.

One example is the maintenance issue of the Plaza Pekeliling building. We used to do a bit of 'fire-fighting' but now we reflect on how to go about certain issues. If we realise that we do not have the expertise to do something, we employ professionals, put them on contract and evaluate their performance. Sometimes we sack them and change contractors to handle the maintenance of the building. This is the result of the AL process. This has not only been done at my level but also by staff in my department. This is slowly transforming them into more independent people.

One of the most important things introduced to the Global Carriers Group is that the Heads of Department now meet regularly with the Board of Directors. Before we introduce changes, the top management team is asked for their opinion because changes affect everybody. So they are given a chance to voice their opinion and as a result they feel they are part of the Group and they have contributed to the idea itself.

Prior to the crisis, we did not reflect on anything that we did. Even when the crisis first hit, we were only 'fire-fighting', by responding to urgent and important issues while ignoring other important activities such as planning and reflection. But after a while we realised, for example, the dry bulk vessels were not making money so we reflected on this and we took the decision to lay them up. However, we still incurred crew expenses. We then reduced to one set of crew so that we could save money because at that time we had a very tight cash flow.

The Crew Manager's response was as follows:

Because of the ARAL process, we have operational meetings and brain-storming sessions which help us to be more effective. Through brain-storming sessions, we realised that all staff need training. From there we decide what type of training they need and then arrange the training.

We have also used the ARAL process to plan the salary structure for staff. We checked with other shipping companies for examples of their salary scales and other benefits, before deciding on our own salary structure.

The Resource Person's views were as follows:

During the Asian economic crisis, I was in touch with the CEO on a regular basis. He kept me informed about how the AR Group was functioning and how they had initiated the forming of the additional AL sets. I visited him and the AR Group Members and gave them reassurance that they were on the right path and encouraged them to continue with their good work.

I am extremely impressed with the impact of the ARAL approach and the type of change that has resulted in the departments and how the department heads have coped with the external environment, especially during the economic crisis.

The CEO had the following comments:

All I can say is that if the senior managers had not been committed to the ARAL approach and had not used the Asian economic crisis as a learning experience, the company would not have survived.

Reflections on Cycle 2

During Cycle 2, the AR Group Members continued with their involvement in the introduction of the change process in the Global Carriers Group using AR. However, the Asian economic crisis had a major impact on the Group. They responded to the crisis very positively by forming a Finance AL Set to deal with the finances of the Group, a Restructuring AL Set to deal with the restructuring of the Group, and an Operations AL Set, which dealt with all the shipping operations.

As a result of the activities of the AL Sets, the Global Carriers Group managed to weather the Asian economic crisis and became more effective and efficient. The ARAL approach therefore benefited the Global Carriers Group as a whole because of the positive changes resulting from the work of the AL Sets.

The chain of evidence in Cycle 2 clearly shows how the AR Group Members coped with this difficult time using the ARAL approach, which resulted in the survival of the Group. The WAL model that emerged in Cycle 2 of this project is summarised in Figure 3.4.

The ARAL model shows the emergence of three separate AL Sets from the AR Group Members. This process was a major learning experience for the CEO (the author of this chapter) and the senior managers (the AR Group Members) as they learnt how to cope in the new turbulent environment.

Figure 3.4 – Cycle 2 WAL Process using ARAL

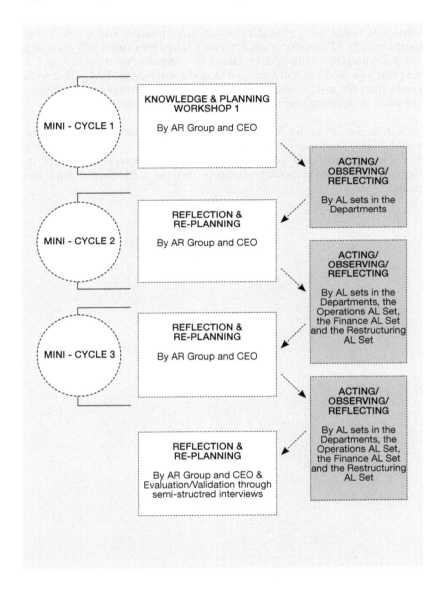

SUMMARY

The AR process in Cycle 1 was made up of four mini-cycles. Each mini-cycle lasted for a period of about three months and Cycle 1 was approximately 12 months in total. Cycle 2 lasted two and a half years and had 3 mini-cycles. Mini-cycle 1 lasted five months, mini-cycle 2 and 3 were one year each. It will be noted that the mini-cycles in Cycle 2 were longer than the mini-cycles in Cycle 1 because the problems were bigger and more demanding and required more time to address.

It can be seen from this WAL program that the demands of the problem would dictate the time frames of the major and mini cycles. The findings of the program clearly point out the positive impact of the ARAL approach on how the senior managers and the CEO coped with the changing times.

CHAPTER 4

MANAGING RE-STRUCTURING & CHANGE — A WAL APPROACH
AN IRC-PNG CASE STUDY
Alois Daton

ABSTRACT

This WAL program involved the development of a strategic business plan and the implementation of restructuring in the Internal Revenue Commission (IRC) of Papua New Guinea to bring about change in the way business was conducted, with the ultimate view of improving the delivery of services. The Action Research method in this program includes two major cycles of planning, acting, observation, reflection/evaluation, and validation. The process of this WAL program can be a useful approach for the managing of change where CEOs and senior managers could enable government departments to explore, devise and implement the required processes of change.

BACKGROUND

The management of the IRC believed that it was necessary for it to undergo organisational and departmental restructuring in order to deliver quality service to the people of PNG. Not only management but staff also were aware of this problem and together saw the need to introduce a change strategy that would review current functions and restructure the organisation to bring about changes to the way business was being conducted.

The change strategy was introduced in IRC through a Work-Applied Learning(WAL) program. The purpose of the WAL program was to establish a strategic business plan for IRC and restructure the IRC through an Action Research (AR) process. This process involved a group of senior managers and the Chief Executive Officer (CEO) as the Action Research Group (ARG).

The facilitator of this program was the Director of Corporate Affairs (Facilitator) who has since been promoted to the Commissioner of Tax. The Facilitator was a senior officer in the organisation and he played a key role in facilitating the ARG as the key group in the planning and implementation of the restructuring.

There was support for this program in that:

- the CEO of the IRC had given approval for the program;
- the site portrayed a rich mix of processes and many senior staff were willing to participate in the program; and
- the Facilitator had prior understanding about the site and had a good working experience of the organisation.

THE ACTION RESEARCH GROUP (ARG)

The ARG was made up of the CEO and senior managers in the IRC. The senior managers had post-graduate qualifications and professional development in Action Research, Action Learning and management. These senior managers had been previously funded by the IRC to undertake a post-graduate qualification in Australia, where they became familiar with change management using AR. As part of their post-graduate studies, they had completed subjects in business and management, including strategic management, change management through Action Research, leadership, human resource management, and Work-Applied Learning facilitation by implementing Work-Based projects. The ARG was responsible for the planning for the following outcomes for IRC: establishment of a strategic business plan and restructuring the organisation; implementing these plans; and observing and reflecting on the progress of these activities.

There were two major cycles, the first for the strategic planning phase and the second for the restructuring phase.

The ARG evaluated outcomes of each major cycle during meetings with the CEO and the Cross Divisional Teams (CDTs). The Facilitator was a participant observer and a member of the ARG. He worked with the CEO and other members of the ARG and the CDTs in developing the strategic business plan and succession plan and implementing the restructuring process using the AR method.

THE CROSS DIVISIONAL TEAMS (CDTS)

The CDTs were Action Learning teams, made up of divisional heads and senior managers of the fourteen Tax, Customs and Corporate Services departments based in Port Moresby. The role of the CDTs was to participate in the review of the strategic business plan and the re-structuring of their respective divisions and to present these details at the CDT meetings. These meetings were also attended by the CEO and ARG members. The CDT meetings were the key forums in the discussion and development of the strategic business plan and the implementation of the restructuring process using the AR method.

VALIDATORS

Internal Validator

The internal validator of the project was the CEO. As the head of the IRC, he was the initiator of the restructuring process and he worked with the Facilitator, members of the ARG and the CDTs to restructure the IRC. He was involved in triangulation of data which was gathered and analysed by the ARG and the CDTs, and he was also the validator of this data, the strategic business plan and the new structure.

External Validators

The Department of Personnel Management (DPM) of PNG was the external validator of data presented to it by the ARG on the development of the strategic business plan and the implementation of the restructuring process.

Another group of external validators were three former Commissioners General of the IRC. They participated in the strategic business planning workshop and were involved as validators for the strategic business plan, the restructuring process and succession planning process.

THE WAL PROGRAM

This restructuring project had two Major Cycles and Mini-Cycles within the Major Cycles. Figure 4.1 illustrates the process in Major Cycles 1 and 2. Figure 4.2 illustrates a typical Mini-Cycle during which the ARG and the CDT developed the strategic business plan and implemented the restructuring process in the IRC.

During Major Cycle 1, the management of the IRC was asked to consider and undertake a review of the organisation's structure. The management team, of which the Facilitator was a member, agreed to undertake the review but before the review could commence, the organisation needed to establish a strategic business plan in respect of its core functions. Major Cycle 1 was over six months and was aimed at the establishment of the strategic business plan. At the end of Major Cycle 1, the ARG members and the CDTs presented the strategic business plan to the former Commissioners General and the CEO as validators of the plan.

Having established and validated the strategic business plan, the IRC management then embarked on the next phase of this change process. Major Cycle 2, which was dealing with the restructure exercise, was much prolonged, due to the unfortunate political and economic upheavals that plagued PNG at the time. In this cycle, the restructured proposal was presented to the DPM and the CEO for their validation and approval.

Figure 4.1 – The AR Process in Major Cycles 1 & 2

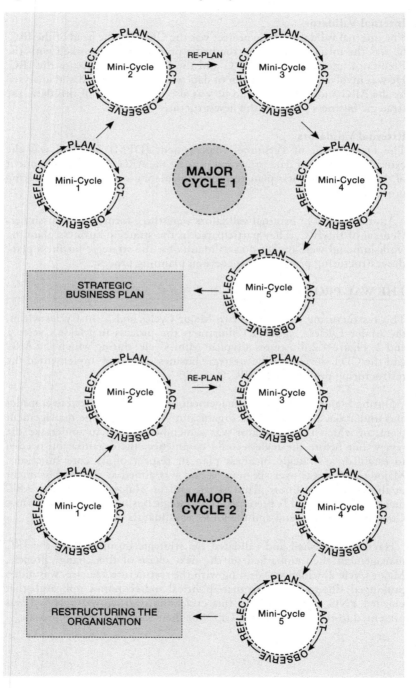

Figure 4.2 – The Typical AR Mini-cycle in a Major Cycle

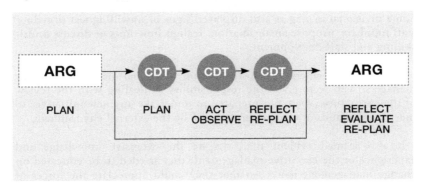

MAJOR CYCLE 1

Major Cycle 1 involved the establishment of the IRC strategic business plan through five Mini-Cycles and these are described in the following sections.

Mini-Cycle 1

The CEO proposed that a steering committee, later to be called the ARG, should take responsibility for investigating and deliberating on major issues of the government's new policy of reduction of staff in the public service and undertake a restructuring process in the organisation. The ARG comprised seven senior managers from the Tax Operations, Customs Operations and the Service Divisions, including the Facilitator. All the ARG members had been sponsored by the IRC to undertake post-graduate studies in Australia using the AR approach.

The first task of the ARG in the implementation of the restructuring process was to establish its role and the role of the stakeholders, which included the AR Group members; the CEO; the Facilitator; the CDTs; and the external validators, namely, the DPM and the former Commissioners- General.

An e-mail from the ARG was issued to all divisional heads about a workshop on the proposed restructuring. It requested the divisional heads to nominate the staff members who should be involved in discussions and the review of their respective divisional structures. Divisions were invited to liaise with the ARG members for assistance regarding any difficulties they faced in the review of their respective divisional structures.

It was during those early months before the proposed workshop that the ARG observed some divisional heads and their staff had little or no idea about how and where to start this review process. Some had sought assistance by discussing the structure during their divisional meetings, while others did not make any approaches to the ARG and its members. Some divisional managers also displayed signs of unwillingness to reduce staff numbers, propose amalgamation, realign functions or discuss multi-skilling and staff development.

The ARG members noted that some divisional heads and senior managers, who were given the responsibility of dealing with the review of their structures, were not prepared to undertake any new initiatives to meet the demands of changes brought on by the external environment.

It also seemed evident that, despite the extensive knowledge and experience of the executive management, they needed to be educated on change management issues, so that they could appreciate the forces of change currently affecting operations, and become agents to bring about new changes.

The ARG discussed these issues with the CEO and agreed that there was a need to deal with the vision, mission, divisional objectives and strategies of IRC and to communicate these issues to the staff.

Mini-Cycle 2

As a result of the problems encountered in Mini-Cycle 1, the CEO issued a memo to the CDTs, informing them of the workshop that would deal firstly with the strategic business plan, secondly with the structure and then with the succession plan. The CDT heads and their managers were required to revisit a previous draft strategic business plan, review their own divisional structures and discuss succession planning to prepare for the workshop. They were also asked to develop their proposals for the vision and mission statements of IRC.

The first CDT meeting was held to discuss the strategic business plan. Thirty divisional heads and their managers and the ARG members attended the meeting which ran for three hours. Customs Operations divisional heads and managers, including their Commissioner, did not attend this meeting.

In the absence of Customs representatives, six proposals of the vision and mission statements of the IRC were presented and the members discussed the proposals, analysed and reflected on the views of the presenters and together they decided on the vision and mission statements which are set out below:

- Vision — to be recognised as highly professional, fair, efficient and innovative.
- Mission — to generate and collect revenue, facilitate economic growth and assist in protecting PNG society.

In addition to establishing the vision and mission of the IRC, the CDTs and ARG members decided to hold another meeting to discuss and establish the divisional objectives and strategies for IRC.

Mini-Cycle 3

A CDT meeting was held for divisional representatives to present their divisional objectives and strategies for discussion. Most divisional representatives presented their objectives and strategies, while some presented only their proposed objectives and a few did not have either ready.

The CDTs analysed the proposals, reflected on the discussion and agreed that all objectives and strategies be sent to the ARG, which would be responsible for reviewing them and discussing any proposed amendments with divisional heads. The ARG would then compile all the submissions from the divisions into one file and place it in Shared Data on the computer network for all staff to have access to and make comments.

The ARG held a meeting on the following day, reflected on the discussions at the CDT meeting the previous day, and agreed to issue a memo to all divisional heads and managers, requesting them to complete the following tasks before attending the next meeting:

- develop or restate their divisional objectives;
- review and refine their divisional strategies; and
- submit to the ARG a list of officers who would participate in the proposed workshop.

The divisions which did not previously present and submit their objectives and strategies submitted them to the ARG. The ARG met on two occasions for three hours each and undertook critical reviews, rearranged submissions, communicated with divisions, provided feedback and put together a draft of all divisional objectives and strategies for presentation at the next meeting.

During the reflections of the ARG, a number of observations were made:

- there was a lack of consultation between divisional heads, managers and their staff in establishing objectives, strategies and action plans;
- there was a lack of understanding of the process of establishing a strategic business plan;
- there was an absence of leadership and direction; and
- the participative process of managing work and learning was becoming evident.

The ARG members discussed the content of the strategic business plan document, which was sent to all divisional heads, and concluded that at the next CDT meeting, a presentation on the process of establishing the vision, mission, objectives and strategies should be delivered for the benefit of all divisional delegates.

The ARG also agreed that during the next CDT meeting, they would discuss matters relating to absences from meetings and better coordination and dissemination of information for their members and staff.

Mini-Cycle 4

The ARG attended a CDT meeting to discuss problems observed in the last three Mini-Cycles.

During this CDT meeting, the ARG presented the draft objectives and strategies of all divisions. Before critical comments and general discussion of the draft objectives and strategies were undertaken, the ARG provided information to the CDT members on strategic planning and clarifying and defining the vision and mission, with particular attention on the objectives and strategies. They also showed staff how to look at the main functions of their divisions and how to identify the primary reasons for their establishment.

The CDT members discussed the objectives and strategies, and divisions were invited to either hand in their drafts to the ARG or take more time to review their submissions before being endorsed at the workshop. Most divisions opted to review their submissions and the meeting agreed to have all revisions submitted to the ARG within the stipulated timeframe.

They encouraged all the CDT members to reflect upon the knowledge of strategic planning in the context of their project.

They agreed on a deadline which allowed the ARG sufficient time to format the strategic business plan document and print copies for at least 60 participants.

Mini-Cycle 5

The ARG met after all final submissions from divisions were received. Each submission was reviewed to ensure that divisional objectives and strategies were correctly presented. The executive officer to the CEO was asked to update the draft strategic business plan by including all new changes and arranging for the printing of 60 copies for the workshop. The ARG also put together a draft workshop program for the CEO's approval. The approved workshop program was circulated to all workshop participants one day before the workshop.

The draft plan was also to include statements by the Minister, reflections of the former Commissioners General, the IRC Profile, Core Values, and the Management Overview.

The strategic business plan workshop was held at Loloata Island Resort, about twenty kilometres down the eastern coast from Port Moresby. Holding the workshop away from the office allowed every member to meaningfully participate and discuss the issues relating to the strategic business plan, restructure and succession planning, without the distractions of day-to-day matters.

The workshop participants were privileged to have in attendance three former Commissioners General of the IRC, namely, Mr John Lohberger, Sir Nagora Bogan and Mr James Loko. They were invited to the, workshop as resource persons and to provide their views on discussions and outcomes of the workshop. They were, to an extent, used as sounding boards during discussions on the three agenda items, and more importantly, were there as validators of the strategic business plan.

The draft layout of the strategic business plan document was completed at the workshop and the contents are set out in Table 4.1.

Table 4.1 – Layout of Strategic Business Plan Document

PAGE	CONTENT	RESPONSIBILITY
Cover	IRC Logo and Title	ARG
1	Foreword by Minister	CEO, Minister
2	Reflections by Past Commissioners Generals	Three former Commissioners General
3	Brief Profile of IRC Beginnings	ARG
4	The Vision	ARG, CDTs
5	The Mission Statement	ARG, CDTs
6	The Core Values	ARG, CDTs
7	IRC Organisation Chart	Internal Affairs Division
8	Management Overview by Commissioner General	CEO
9 – 15	Divisional Objectives and Strategies	CDTs

The ARG members were facilitators of the workshop. The draft strategic business plan was presented and the workshop participants were taken through the entire draft document. Discussion then took place with contributions from members and the three former Commissioner Generals. A brainstorming exercise was undertaken to establish the core values for the IRC and these core values are set out in Table 4.2.

Table 4.2 – The IRC Core Values

	CORE VALUES
1	We must uphold the integrity, impartiality and fairness of the tax system.
2	We must correctly apply the tax law so that all our customers are provided fair and equal treatment.
3	We must take pride in our work and carry out our duties professionally.
4	We must learn to work in teams, empower our staff and be diligent in our efforts so that quality service is provided to our clients.
5	We must build trust and respect for each other and value individual differences of our staff and clients.
6	We must be honest and transparent in our dealings with each other and our clients and be held accountable for our actions.
7	We must recognise efforts of staff, give credit where it is due and reward them accordingly.
8	We must build an environment that will provide equal opportunity for all staff, including minority groups.
9	We must work through each other, with each other, and for each other with commitment and strive for excellence in all we do.
10	We must be prepared to adapt to environmental changes and implement change where appropriate.

With the core values in place, the only other contributions to the plan were a brief statement from the Prime Minister, a statement from each of the three former Commissioners General, and a brief profile of the IRC. The ARG was requested to obtain these items to complete the strategic business plan. The Loloata meeting then endorsed the plan which was validated by the three former Commissioners General.

The document was expected to be finalised, proofread and ready for printing towards the end of the year and expected to be launched by the Prime Minister.

The restructure agenda was then raised and discussed, and the workshop participants resolved that the ARG would lead the way in co-ordinating meetings and activities to restructure the organisation in the near future.

The final item discussed at the workshop was succession planning. The participants were told that succession planning was a concept to develop the management skills of managers and senior staff at all levels. Succession planning would contribute to the appointment of staff to acting positions when their supervisors moved into higher positions or elsewhere in the organisation. The concept was validated and again the ARG was given the responsibility of leading the planning and related activities for its publicity, discussion, implications on resources availability, vetting by management and subsequent implementation.

The completion of the strategic business plan process was a major achievement for the organisation and all the participants who attended the lead-up meetings and the workshop were pleased with the outcome. For the first time in a long while, the IRC had put in place strategies to use in working towards the organisation's primary objective of revenue generation and collection.

The mission and achievable goals were defined with the establishment of the core values from which executive managers could inspire staff to perform to expected standards and beyond. The strategic business plan was also validated by the three former Commissioners General and this now paved the way for the IRC to introduce other change initiatives such as the review of the structure and succession planning.

In summary, this final Mini-Cycle of Major Cycle 1 saw the establishment of the IRC strategic business plan. The cycles of planning, acting, observation and reflection occurred at the level of the CDTs and ARG. The data that was captured through this cycle was triangulated and validated by the CDT, ARG, the current CEO, and by the three former Commissioners General at the workshop.

MAJOR CYCLE 2

Following the development of the strategic business plan, Major Cycle 2 got under way, which involved the implementation of the restructuring process over five Mini-Cycles.

The details of these Mini-Cycles are in the following sections.

Mini-Cycle 1

A meeting between the Facilitator, the CEO and his executive officer was held, when the CEO asked for the ARG to begin work on the restructuring process. He asked that the idea of merging small divisions with larger divisions which have like functions be considered. The ARG met to discuss the suggestion and a number of options were arrived at which are set out in Table 4.3. Concepts and models of restructuring in organisations was presented by the Facilitator and reflected upon with the ARG in the context of IRC's restructuring.

Table 4.3 – Change Proposal

PROPOSAL OPTIONS		
Activities	**Re-arrangement and Re-allocation of Positions**	**Amalgamate Service Divisions**
1	Disband Revenue Management division and transfer functions to Enforcement, Resource Monitoring and Regional Operations divisions	Create a new division of Corporate Services comprising Corporate Affairs, Human Resources and Information Technology
2	Re-allocate all positions, except for the Assistant Commissioner, to Resource Monitoring, Enforcement and Regional Operations divisions	Amalgamate Corporate Affairs and Human Resources into one division
3	Review and amend all duty statements	Transfer position of Assistant Commissioner Revenue Management to the new division of Corporate Services
4	Transfer staff of the disbanded Revenue Management division to the three divisions mentioned in point 2 above.	Review and amend duty statements to reflect functions, responsibilities and lines of reporting

The ARG noted that the proposed restructuring needed the approval of the DPM, being the government department responsible for policy matters on recruitment, conditions of employment and staff welfare in the PNG public service.

The ARG agreed to prepare a submission to seek approval from the DPM for the proposed changes and forward it to the CEO for his consideration. The issues that were addressed in the submission are set out in Table 4.4.

Table 4.4 – Issues in submission to DPM

ISSUES	
A	The purpose
B	Background
C	Scope of the review
D	Current structure of Revenue Management
E	Details of Revenue Management functions
F	Proposed new division of Corporate Services
G	Proposed re-arrangement of functions — The Four Options
H	Management reporting — line of communication
I	Implementation plan
J	Implementation concern
K	Conclusion

The ARG noted that over a period of more than twelve months, there would have to be a number of meetings to deal with the restructure of the IRC or at least some areas of it. During that time, submissions and recommendations would be sent to the CEO for comment and decisions.

The Facilitator advised the ARG that he would like to focus on training and developing skills of staff for succession to senior positions during the following year. The ARG noted that at meetings with the CEO, he had plans for changes to take place in IRC, but the demands of his position made it difficult for him to allocate time for this.

In this Mini-Cycle, the facilitator, the CEO and the ARG members met, reflected on changes, planned and commenced work on implementing the restructuring process. The ARG members observed and reflected on meetings with the CEO and events which had transpired during the course of the cycle. Rearrangements to positions in two operational areas were made as part of the restructuring process and were sent to the CEO for endorsement.

Mini-Cycle 2

Two years after the development of the strategic business plan, the submission to the DPM was awaiting the CEO's approval.

A management meeting was held and one of the agenda items was the restructuring of the IRC. It was agreed that work on the restructure should be commenced and the ARG was tasked with facilitating the restructuring exercise.

The ARG agreed to conduct monthly meetings with divisional heads, their senior managers and officers to discuss issues on the structure and to have regular meetings with senior management to provide progress updates.

A presentation was considered essential to inform CDT members about the objectives of reforms, instruments of reforms, reform issues in the IRC, and related issues. The ARG was of the view that divisions should have to take a holistic approach to restructuring their sections. Details provided in the presentation would assist divisions in working on issues that were commonly shared across the organisation and others which might be overlooked as divisions competed against each other for maximum benefit.

A CDT meeting was attended by about 30 divisional heads and managers. The CEO had to attend a Cabinet meeting and sent his apology. The Commissioner for Customs did not attend and the Commissioner for Tax arrived after the meeting had started.

The Facilitator opened the meeting and informed the participants that the purpose of the meeting was to discuss the ways in which a restructure exercise could be undertaken in order to make the IRC an efficient government service deliverer.

The former government had embarked on a reform program for the Public Service and the recently elected government would likely continue with the program, given the current economic and political situation in the country.

The Facilitator told the meeting that the ARG had arranged for a brief presentation to stimulate thinking and encourage active contributions towards a strategy of reforms and change with the aim of enabling the restructuring exercise to achieve overall government reform objectives.

At the conclusion of the presentation, questions were asked and general discussion took place. The ARG members met after the meeting to evaluate the outcome of the meeting. The points raised were as follows:

- It was disappointing not to have the CEO open the meeting and set the direction for discussion.
- It was obvious that divisions had not looked beyond their own areas.
- There was resistance for the restructuring exercise.
- Foreign expatriates and one national were either dominant in their discussions with their staff, dictated terms of discussion, or did not discuss the matter at all. The Melanesian cultural concept of "respect and loyalty" for elders and leaders may have inhibited the managers and lower ranking staff.
- This attitude was noted in restructure meetings where divisional heads had been dominant while managers and other divisional staff had contributed very little by way of discussions.
- The discussions had helped some participants to look at restructuring in a holistic manner.
- The presentation was therefore considered very educational, and to an extent popular, with more staff wanting access to the information.
- The ARG wanted the positive momentum of the discussions for restructure to continue and they decided to meet with the CEO to discuss this issue.

The ARG decided to meet the CEO to discuss the problems which were affecting the progress of the restructuring process. The issues for discussion included the CEO's absence at the last CDT meeting, delay in responding to memos and submissions from the ARG, absence of leadership for the restructuring process, resistance to change, and lack of communication, commitment and discipline.

Mini-Cycle 3

Although the ARG members could not meet the CEO because of his commitments, they began to discuss among themselves the need to have in place draft restructure models. This was necessary in the event that divisions came up with many different models and failed to agree on a common model, or had nothing in place to offer. The first model discussed was to restructure by functions.

The Facilitator, the Executive Officer to the CEO and the Manager for Human Resources met and briefed the CEO on the first restructure meeting. A brief containing a summary of the discussions and end of meeting evaluations by the ARG was handed to the CEO and he was advised that the date of the second restructure meeting would not be announced until this briefing document had been seen by the CEO. The CEO was brought up to date on what had happened so far and was advised that the ARG needed his views and firm announcements of the direction he intended to take.

The CEO scanned the brief, including the evaluations, and considered the problems of implementing the restructuring process. He apologised for not being at the first restructure meeting and for devoting little time and support to the ARG. However, he urged members to continue with the work undertaken so far and pledged to deal with the problems at the next CDT meeting.

The next issue discussed was the strategy to deal with the intended notice to all divisional heads and managers for the next restructure meeting. The CEO wanted the notice to include provoking questions such as amalgamation of like functions, outsourcing, multi-skilling, performance management, use of staff skills, and resources. He was advised that most of these issues had been discussed at the first restructure meeting and details of the presentation by the ARG had been placed on Shared Data at the request of those who participated.

It was agreed that the ARG would develop a set of questions for staff to consider when undertaking restructuring activities. The CEO suggested that the questions be developed and included as part of a memo to all staff so that they could use the questions as a guide.

The ARG then met to develop a set of provoking questions for stimulating discussion among staff when they discussed proposals for a new structure of the IRC.

The ARG members discussed the current structure and suggested amalgamating functions which crossed divisional boundaries like assessing, audits, accounting, advising, enforcement and compliance. Discussion took place on the possibilities of outsourcing certain enforcement functions, such as surveillance and intelligence gathering, which could be best performed by the Police Department and the Defence Force.

The members also discussed the possibility of outsourcing certain functions of the Information Technology division such as maintenance of hardware and certain programs, apart from the Revenue Accounting System.

Other issues discussed were:

- multi-skilling staff to perform more than one function;
- amalgamating receipting and accounting functions;
- sharing of resources in the provincial offices;
- having one tax file number for all accounts per taxpayer;
- cutting out duplication of functions; and
- relinquishing functions which fall under other jurisdictions, such as Racing and Gaming, to the National Gaming Control Board.

From the deliberations on the above issues, the ARG developed a number of questions and these were included in a memo to all staff, which was to be approved by the CEO.

The second restructure meeting was attended by almost 50 staff members comprising executive managers and senior staff of Customs Operations, Tax Operations and the Service divisions. The CEO also attended and formally opened the meeting.

His opening remarks were focused on the purpose of the meeting, which was for the three operational areas to present their restructure proposals and for the participants to discuss these proposals. Restructuring the IRC as part of government reforms was a long term response to government support. The CEO said the present structure may not be adequate and all staff needed to be considerate of all parameters affecting the IRC, such as resourcing and the capacity of staff to manage operations. In the course of planning restructuring activities, he encouraged everyone to look for economies of scale across the whole organisation, not just their own individual divisions.

The future structure should make the organisation look smaller and fit within the staffing ceiling and budget. It must make sense by creating career paths for all positions. Serious consideration should be given to the current structure and its functions, and staff should establish what problems exist and how they should be dealt with. Restructuring should help the organisation deliver services better and more effectively, but it is not the key to prudent management. All officers have to consider capacity building, equip staff with the necessary skills to manage human resources, systems and procedures, build up leadership skills and commence succession planning.

He urged the participants to listen to the presentations and then undertake meaningful discussion considering the contributions of everyone. This would lead to a new structure that would benefit staff, stakeholders and the people of PNG.

The CEO then referred to the problems affecting the restructuring process that had been noted by the ARG and discussed with him. He asked staff for their total commitment to the restructuring process, to improve attendance at meetings, to look at the restructuring in an holistic manner and to look at the benefits to the organisation and the staff in the long term.

Representatives of all the divisions were then asked to present their proposals and a very lively debate was held on restructuring issues.

As the participants had agreed to defer discussion of the proposal to the next meeting, it was agreed that the ARG would set a date for the next meeting once all proposals were received.

Mini-Cycle 4

The ARG members had a brief meeting, with the exception of the Assistant Commissioner for Resource Monitoring who was attending another appointment. The meeting was called to evaluate discussions of the second restructure meeting.

The meeting started out as planned, with the CEO and the two Commissioners General present. The CEO, however, had to leave to attend a Cabinet meeting and therefore was unable to see all the presentations. The members agreed that it was important that the CEO participate in the discussions of the proposed structure so that he could become more involved in shaping the new structure. The ARG hoped his commitments and schedule allowed for this to happen.

A number of staff members left the meeting venue before the last presentation was completed because they had other engagements. The ARG agreed that meetings of this nature should be held away from the office so that all participants make their contributions without disruption. However, in view of the financial situation of the country and the limited funding to hire external conference facilities, it was agreed that all future meetings that year would continue to be held in the office.

The Facilitator met briefly with the CEO after the ARG meeting and informed him of the date of the third restructure meeting. The Tax Operations division would present its restructure proposal at this meeting, which would then be followed by discussion of the three proposals. The discussions from this meeting should point to solid directions in which the new structure would be finalised.

The CEO suggested that the third restructure meeting be held outside of the office and this meeting should be for the endorsement of the new structure. Apart from the restructure, there was a need to also discuss the strategic business plan, as the interim plan ran to the end of that year and there was a need to look at establishing a new one for the next five years. It would be more appropriate for this plan to be based on the new structure.

The third restructure meeting was attended by 20 divisional heads and senior managers, including ARG members. The number in attendance was slightly low due to some managers and senior staff taking annual leave. The CEO and the Commissioner for Customs Operations were attending meetings outside of the office and were not able to attend. The Commissioner for Tax Operations was on leave and so the Assistant Commissioner for Revenue Collection represented Tax Operations as well as his own division.

In the absence of the CEO, the Facilitator opened the meeting and reiterated what the CEO had said at the last meeting on achieving a leaner structure, attaining improved efficiency, creating career paths and building institutional capacity. Customs Operations and the Service divisions had already presented their restructure models and this meeting would see Tax Operations present their proposal. Discussion would then be undertaken on all three proposals.

The Assistant Commissioner for Revenue Collection presented the restructure proposal for Taxation Operations, and discussions were held on all the three proposals. From the three proposals, there appeared to be overwhelming support for the Service divisions to report to one Assistant Commissioner.

The ARG then met to discuss observations and evaluate the proceedings of the third restructure meeting. The meeting was attended by all members except the Executive Officer to the CEO who was away on recreation leave. The observations of the ARG included the following:

-   The ARG was expected to develop a model that encompassed all the agreements and differences that resulted from the discussions of the third restructure meeting.
-   It was noted that Customs Operations were more receptive to change and their proposal ensured that the executive management positions made little or no reference to Customs or Tax.
-   Tax Operations were more resistant to change and opposed mergers of assessing and audit functions of the organisation and wanted the restructure along business lines.
-   The next restructure meeting needed to review and clearly set out the functions of the organisation; mergers and segregation of functions can then be undertaken and a new structure derived from this.
-   The ARG still had not been informed of the reason for the delay by the CEO in announcing the approval of the new structure of the Service divisions.

In discussing the above observations, the ARG invited the Assistant Commissioner for Resource Monitoring to defend the resistance displayed by Tax Operations. He stressed that they wanted to keep the assessing and audit functions out of the proposed mergers, because of the complex nature of assessing tax returns of resource companies and large businesses, and undertaking audits of the accounts of these companies. The auditors in his division were trained to deal with large companies and they needed to be kept in that group to deal with complex cases.

Auditors in other areas like Source Collection and VAT performed tasks which had different levels of complexities from each other and auditors from Resource Monitoring and Revenue Assessment divisions also had different levels of complexities. They therefore proposed a name change for the Resource Monitoring division to International and Large Businesses.

The ARG then looked at a possible model and it was decided that if there was to be a presentation of a model at the next meeting, the ARG needed to develop something that would give the organisation a new look and a fresh image, different from the current structure.

The ARG's view was to look beyond changing names of positions by developing a radical structure that was worth the time and effort of all staff involved in the exercise. The discussions culminated in Restructure Model A and Restructure Model B, which are shown as Figures 4.3 and 4.4. These were to be presented at the next restructure meeting.

Figure 4.3 – Restructure Model A

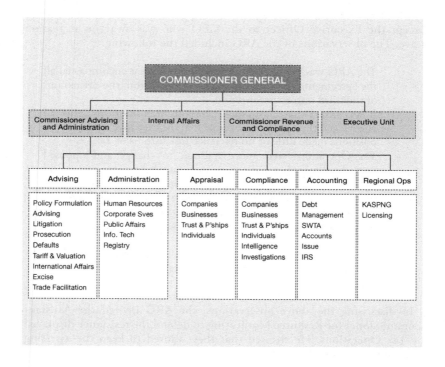

Figure 4.4 – Restructure Model B

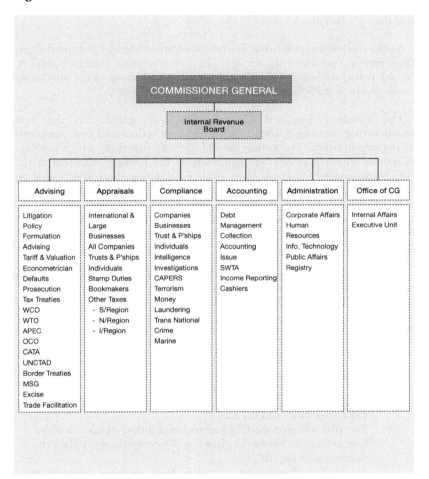

The ARG met, with the exception of the Director of Resource Monitoring, to discuss the proposed models and the need to review divisional objectives and the core functions.

As the models were showing the proposed structure by functional lines, there were no positions shown after the Commissioner level in Model A. Model B had included a Board and was a radical move never previously envisaged in any PNG government department structure.

The members discussed the functions and agreed that the next restructuring meeting needed to review the objectives and core functions of the organisation. The review should identify functions which overlap, functions which may not be significant to the primary business of the IRC, functions which could be outsourced and functions which may no longer be appropriate as part of the organisation's core business.

The ARG agreed that the best people to undertake the review were the divisional heads and their staff and this should be the main agenda of the next restructure meeting.

The ARG raised issues in relation to Model B and asked for an explanation of the role of the Internal Revenue Board (IRB). The ensuing discussions noted that the IRB replaced the positions of the Commissioners, and comprised a number of divisional heads directly below the Board. A number of functions were proposed for the Board as follows:

- The IRB will be responsible for managing the operations of the IRC.
- The IRB will deal with all submissions in relation to technical, operational, disciplinary and administrative matters and make recommendations to the CEO.
- The IRB will free the CEO of responsibilities, which will allow him to focus on his role of planning, directing and controlling the operations of the IRC.
- The IRB will meet on a regular basis, possibly once every two weeks.

The ARG also discussed the need to be familiar with the details of the models and justify why the models were presented along functional lines. This was necessary in order to answer any questions raised by participants at the next restructure meeting. It was agreed that an ARG meeting would be called in the next seven days to deal with this matter.

The ARG members met again to discuss answers to questions that may be asked by CDT members in relation to the two proposed restructure models. The questions discussed are as follows:

Q1. Why should the proposed structure be modelled along functional lines?

    A1. A structure can be designed either by location, matrix form or functional lines.

    For the IRC to restructure by location, it would be necessary to provide facilities to accommodate officers in the provinces in areas such as assessing, auditing, advising and, to a certain extent, enforcement. Officers in these areas were currently operating from Port Moresby. The IRC would also need to create client files for each location and establish revenue collection, accounting and reporting systems for each main location.

    Restructuring by location was possible and the IRC could consider the Australian Tax Office establishment where each Australian State has a chief executive officer who reports to the Commissioner in Canberra.

    To be able to restructure in this manner, IRC would require resources above its normal annual budget appropriation and possible assistance by way of external aid. All executive and decision making authority currently rested with management in Port Moresby and it would require significant education for executive staff members in change management processes, commitment and change of attitude to take on a new change issue. Funding of infrastructure and logistics makes restructuring by location not a favoured option.

    A2. To restructure by matrix would be difficult for the IRC because of the line of reporting. Officers in Customs and VAT in the provinces would see them reporting to the Regional Director in their province and also to their Assistant Commissioner in Port Moresby.

    Given that management decisions for the Enforcement Division were made by the Assistant Commissioner in Port Moresby, and not the Regional Director in the province, the ARG saw the inadequacy of communication procedures and line of reporting as a disadvantage for the matrix approach.

A3. The restructuring along functional lines would be convenient to achieve the objectives and primary mission of the IRC. Apart from advising and administrative support services, there were four main functions which crossed divisional boundaries. These relate to creating tax liability, collecting, accounting and reporting revenue, conducting audits and enforcement activities for compliance and trade facilitation. It would be convenient to merge and amalgamate like functions in order to save costs and multi-skill officers to carry out more than one function.

Q2. Why change names of divisions?

A. The change of division names and titles falls in line with the structure being a new one. The restructure must be seen as a new initiative and when a new change is introduced, the most effective way to convince staff and to gain acceptance and support for the change is to change those things that are associated with the old structure. The change in names of the major functions was seen as the most appropriate approach to sell the proposed structure to the staff members.

Q3. Why create an Internal Revenue Board?

A. The purpose of the Board, which could be called a different name other than a Board, is to improve the performance of the organisation through identification of best practice work processes and systems. The IRC should work in partnership with its clients by providing membership to the Board, through representation from key government departments, the business sector, academics, non-government organisations and stakeholders who have an interest in seeing the IRC provide improved services.

The members discussed the attendance and participation of executive managers at the three restructure meetings and agreed to take the two models to a meeting with the CEO and the two Commissioners General. The models would be presented to them to seek their views, as the ARG needed their support to drive this new change initiative. The members did not want to see a situation where there was disagreement by members of the executive management, and this concern being expressed at a future restructure meeting attended by divisional heads and managers.

The Facilitator told the ARG members that he would be away for four weeks and they indicated that the proposed meeting with the executive management would be held as soon as he returned.

Mini-Cycle 5

The ARG met with the CEO and discussed the restructure as no progress appeared to have been made for almost six months. One of the delays was attributed to a World Bank (WB) funded capacity building program for compliance in Tax Operations. Part of the capacity building program required Tax Operations to review and adjust its current structure. Tax Operations had proposed certain adjustments and presented its proposals to senior managers of the IRC. This had confused a lot of senior managers in Customs Operations and the Service divisions as they had not been fully informed of the WB project and did not know which restructure exercise to deal with.

Another restructure meeting was planned and attended by all CDT members. The purpose of the meeting was twofold. Firstly, it was to allow the ARG to present the two restructure models A and B which had been designed from divisional restructure proposals presented in the previous three CDT meetings. Secondly, it was to allow participants to make critical comments, provide feedback and make recommendations on the future structure of the IRC.

The presentation of the two models created considerable discussion and comments from all participants. There was a general tendency to lean towards Model B. In both models, each area of operation was grouped together under like functions. In Model B, a Board was proposed to oversee and offer advice to the executive management but with no statutory powers.

The meeting reflected on the discussions and noted the following:

- before any decision is made to adopt a model, the divisional delegates must review their core business functions;
- the restructure should consider merging the more generalised functions like collections, accounting and intelligence while Customs and Tax functions remain separate;
- advising should be kept under three categories of government, staff and client;
- if like functions were to be merged, there must be multi-skilling of officers; and
- IRC should apply commonly used names and terms.

The meeting agreed that all divisions should re-examine their core business functions and see where they fit into the model as the previous business plan had been completed three years previously and many new developments had taken place since then. This was done and the ARG submitted the final structure to the CEO, who unofficially shared the developments of the restructuring process with the DPM and reported that the discussions indicated that there was no major objection by the DPM to the IRC plans.

In PNG this is the normal procedure for validation, a process which includes initial comments and then the final approval.

This was the final Mini-Cycle of the program and saw the CEO and members of the ARG and CDT decide on the organisational structure that would be used to carry out its core functions.

REFLECTIONS

The purpose of the WAL program was to:

1. develop a strategic business plan for the IRC;
2. implement the restructuring of the IRC, including succession planning; and
3. undertake the above activities using an AR approach.

PROJECT OUTCOMES

This WAL program proved that change can be introduced with the full participation of staff at all levels of the organisation. The WAL program at the IRC achieved the following project outcomes:

-   it dealt with problems and developed a business plan and a structure for the IRC;
-   it has proven itself as one organisation in which executive managers, divisional heads, senior managers and their staff came to develop a better understanding of their roles and thus improve work practices;
-   it has led to better learning;
-   it has helped to build stronger collegial relationships within the organisation;
-   it has helped to develop a greater understanding and appreciation of the ethics involved in public service work practices;
-   it has broken down some of the hierarchical barriers that separate executive management and other staff;
-   it has provided alternative ways of viewing and approaching work problems with new ways of seeing work practices; and
-   it has helped to examine the 'habits' that have developed — what staff are 'really' doing in the work situation or in management practices.

LEARNING OUTCOMES

There are lessons to be learnt in this WAL program using AR in the context of individual learning, group learning and organisational learning which have impacted on organisational change.

LESSONS FROM PROBLEMS ENCOUNTERED

The problems identified and solved during the WAL program are provided in this section.

Communication
It was noted that the CDT members and their senior officers did not adequately consult with each other and their staff to seek meaningful contributions towards the establishment of the strategic business plan and implementing the restructuring process. This resulted in the following problems:

- lack of knowledge on how to undertake the review of the business plan and the structure;
- resistance to change;
- lack of understanding of change management issues;
- lack of consultation between CDT members and their staff; and
- disagreement among divisional delegates on issues discussed at CDT meetings.

These problems were noted and discussed by the ARG. It was agreed that divisional heads had to take responsibility to disseminate information and inform staff of the changes taking place, since staff members who were fully informed would contribute meaningfully to discussions towards the establishment of the strategic business plan and implementation of the restructuring process.

Selected members of the ARG then met with members of the CDTs and reflected on the problems with them. The CDT members realised that change initiatives needed to be discussed with their staff, informing them of the reasons for the changes, what effect the changes would have and the benefits for staff and the organisation.

The ARG then discussed this matter with the CEO and asked him to raise it at the CDT meeting. This was done and improvement among most of the CDTs was evident in subsequent meetings.

Commitment
The level of commitment from members of the CDTs was good; however, there were problems on a number of occasions and these related to:

- late arrivals and early departures from meetings;
- absences from meetings;
- attendance at meetings but being unprepared;
- delays in submitting restructure proposals; and
- lack of self-discipline

These problems were observed by the ARG and, like the communication problems, it was noted that divisional heads and senior managers were not fulfilling their managerial responsibilities of managing attendance and discipline. The ARG met and discussed the problems and it was noted that commitment was an issue affecting work in all divisions of the IRC.

The ARG then discussed the issue with members of the CDT and requested that they show commitment for the benefits that stand to be gained from the work being undertaken. The ARG also discussed the matter with the CEO and proposed that he raise the matter at a management meeting so that information could be relayed to all staff. The CEO then raised this matter, together with the issue on communication, at the next management meeting, and improvement was evident in subsequent CDT meetings.

External

During the course of the study, there emerged a number of problems from the external environment which affected the progress of the work being undertaken by the ARG and the CDT members. These problems related to:

- the declining state of the country's economy;
- World Bank funded capacity building assistance program for Tax Operations;
- aid assistance from the Government of Australia through the Australian Taxation Office;
- the 2002 national elections; and
- the constitutional legality challenge of the Value Added Tax.

The CEO delegated his responsibility to the Facilitator and advised the ARG and the CDT of the Facilitator's new responsibility.

Cultural

The problems associated with communication and commitments are linked to the attitude and behaviour of members of the CDTs. The cultural impact on the WAL program resulted from two types of influences: i) the 'wantok'; and ii) expatriate influence.

  i) The 'wantok'

The attitudes of members of the CDTs were driven by the Melanesian norm of respect for leaders and support of each other in good and bad times. The problems relating to communication and commitment are behavioural and the 'wantok' features prominently. If, for example, the benefits of the strategic business plan and the implementation of the restructuring process are a threat to the comfort zone of divisional heads and senior managers, change resistance will be a pact struck by CDT members. The 'wantok' influence is essentially support for the group and has consequences for some or all of the issues mentioned under communication and commitment above.

The ARG discussed these cultural issues with CDT members and later with the CEO. The solution suggested was firstly to inform all staff of the vision, mission and goals of the organisation, the benefits that stand to be achieved and that through working in teams, problems can be resolved and benefits achieved. The second suggested solution was for executive management, through Human Resource officers, to promote awareness of team work and striking a balance between the Melanesian culture and the influences of the Western world.

ii)   Expatriate influence

Expatriate officers employed in the IRC as well as those in other government organisations have a large influence on the way business is conducted. The Melanesian culture of showing respect for leaders is practised by many national employees and the impact of this influence is a problem in the attitude and behaviour of staff.

Expatriates ending their contracts in PNG and returning to their previous positions in their own countries have a lot to lose in terms of status and benefits. Therefore the tendency for expatriates is to hold on to their positions for as long as they can, with the result that most of these expatriates are not interested in developing and encouraging the nationals to grow in their jobs.

There was therefore the very subtle tendency by some members of the expatriate population to imply to their fellow divisional managers the lack of importance of this process. Such behaviour invariably impacted upon the loyalty of the subordinates of these expatriate divisional managers in the CDTs. This in turn affected their commitment and passion for the change process.

The ARG informed the CEO of this problem and advised him that he would need to reflect with the expatriates on their commitment to this project. Such a dialogue took place on more than one occasion and it was noted that as the Mini-Cycles evolved from Major Cycles 1 and 2, the expatriates realised that they had to be part of the team and be dedicated and committed to the process.

POSITIVE LESSONS

The positive outcomes that emerged during the implementation of the restructuring process are recorded in this section.

Despite the problems outlined in the previous sections, there were positive outcomes for the staff members who participated in the restructuring process using the AR method.

There were also positive outcomes for the organisation during the restructuring process. The benefits for members of the ARG and the CDT related to working in teams, learning from each other, broadening their perspective beyond their own functional realms and building their confidence in decision making and leadership roles.

This was attributed to the continuous evaluation of outcomes in each cycle where problems were encountered and plans were made to take corrective action to deal with them. The learning and development process for all staff involved emerged throughout the entire process and the consequential benefits were evident. This WAL program has proventhat change can be introduced in the IRC and in government departments in PNG using the AR method for problem solving and knowledge development. Other organisational outcomes are:

- the development and subsequent evaluation and validation of the strategic business plan by all stakeholders;
- a structure designed along functional lines resulting in the major revenue generating functions of assessment, collection and accounting, and enforcement in both Tax and Customs Operations being brought under one relevant division. Divisions have also been renamed as part of the new structure changes;
- a Board reporting to the CEO is a radical approach to change management in the PNG Public Service. This change was considered as the Board would comprise senior executives from key government departments, the economic sector, law and justice, academic institutions, non-government organisations and other key stakeholders with expertise who would identify best practices of getting work done and delivering improved client service; and
- a mooted consequential outcome of the above two changes was the expected support from the government to establish a governing Act for the IRC to "merge" Customs and Tax Operations and subsequently be accorded autonomy. Self-governance will allow the IRC to use program budgeting effectively for operational costs from funds retained from a percentage of revenue collections and would also allow management to have the flexibility to make and manage structural and operational changes brought on by environmental forces (Snyder, Dowd & Houghton 1994).

STAFF OUTCOMES

The WAL program:

- led to better understanding and improved work practices;
- helped to build stronger collegial relationships with others in the organisation;
- helped to develop a greater understanding and appreciation of the ethics involved in public service work practices;

- broke down some of the hierarchical barriers that separate executive management and other staff; and
- helped staff learn about Action Research and developed competence and confidence with change management.

LESSONS LEARNED FROM CEO'S INVOLVEMENT

The CEO's involvement impacted upon the restructuring process and is recorded in this section.

There were many instances throughout the restructuring process where the ARG commented on the participation and commitment of the CEO in providing leadership for the restructuring of the organisation. The need for restructuring the IRC was a change forced by events in the external environment which was supported by the CEO and where he successfully obtained approval from the management to endorse the review of the structure.

He appointed the ARG to lead the restructure process and was made aware throughout the restructure process of the frustrations and delays in moving consistently ahead with the establishment of the strategic business plan and implementing the restructuring process.

The problems were raised with the CEO and relate to:

- absences from meetings;
- delays in decision making;
- communication; and
- leadership.

Absences from meetings

In relation to absences from scheduled meetings, the CEO was on a number of occasions called in for briefings with the Minister and he was required to attend Cabinet meetings during and after the formation of the new government following national elections. Some of these meetings were in conflict with the scheduled ARG and CDT meeting dates, but the CEO had to absent himself in order to provide briefings on the functions and operations of the IRC for the benefit of the incoming Minister and members of the newly elected government.

Selected members of the ARG met with the CEO and raised the issue of absences. He pledged to improve his attendance and was able to attend some of the later meetings of the ARG and CDT.

Delays in decision making

The ARG members expressed to the CEO the frustrations that were experienced because of delays in response to ARG memos and submissions relating to the strategic business plan and implementation of the restructuring process. The CEO attributed the delays to his commitments with the Minister, government and in overseas discussions for aid assistance with the Australian Government.

He eventually relayed his decisions on all the outstanding memos and submissions and made all later decisions in reasonable time for the ARG to proceed with the strategic business plan and the restructuring process.

Communication

The communication problem was discussed with the CEO and he attributed this to his absences from the meetings and commitments mentioned above. He assured the ARG members of his commitment to improved communication, and so in subsequent meetings with members of the ARG and the CDT he was able to inform everyone of all the developments related to the business plan, the restructuring process and aid assistance discussions with the Australian Government.

Leadership

The ARG members met the CEO and pointed out the need for direction of the business plan and the restructuring process, including succession planning as these were change issues to be driven by him.

Change is to be driven by senior management and the process must involve managers and key people at all levels so that the purpose and outcomes are clearly communicated to all staff.

For the same reasons provided in response to the first three problems, the CEO attended and chaired a number of CDT meetings and provided the kind of leadership members of the ARG, CDT and all staff had expected from him.

DELEGATION BY THE CEO TO THE FACILITATOR

The role of the Facilitator in this WAL program was to observe and be a stakeholder in the process of establishing the strategic business plan and the restructure of the public sector organisation, including succession planning, using the AR method.

The Facilitator worked closely with the CEO, and with members of the ARG and CDTs, to resolve the two problems. His role was:
- facilitator;
- member of the ARG; and
- participant observer.

As a delegate of the CEO, the Facilitator was:
- leader; and
- adviser.

There were issues that emerged throughout the WAL program where intervention was only possible by the authority of the CEO or by his two deputies as delegated. Due to the turbulent and uncertain nature of conditions in the PNG Public Service, the CEO and his two deputies were not able to attend meetings with members of the ARG and CDTs to discuss the strategic business plan and the restructure and provide advice and lead the change process.

Due to the above situations, the Facilitator did not undertake the traditional tasks of facilitator and participant observer. Instead, he took on the additional responsibility of being the leader and advisor in the absence of the CEO and his two deputies. The Facilitator played a dominant role in a number of meetings and, as a consequence, provided advice and held discussions with the ARG and the CDTs while at all times ensuring that the degree of his influence was not a major part of the decisions made by these groups.

This invariably led to complications as the ARG members and the CDTs did not accept the Facilitator in this leadership role. This resulted in meetings at times being cancelled because these stakeholders wanted the presence of the CEO to validate decisions.

It also affected the Facilitator's role as a participant observer and impacted upon the relationship between the Facilitator and these stakeholders. The Facilitator had to spend time building up goodwill with these stakeholders on the occasions when he had to play the role of the leader.

This aligns with the concept that managers need to be leaders and the catalysts for change (Kincaide 1997). Successful commitment to change occurs when elected leaders know how to lead, manage, direct, support or enable, and this level of management and leadership is absolutely critical for change.

The CEO did not fully play his role as a catalyst of change in the restructuring process of the public sector organisation using the AR process. This, in fact, was the major reason why the restructuring process took three and a half years to complete.

SUMMARY

The WAL program focused on the development of a strategic business plan and the restructuring of the IRC, including succession planning. It involved the participation and contribution of members of the CDTs and their staff, and the support of the executive management of the IRC under prevailing conditions.

This WAL program demonstrated the challenges of introducing change when there was a critical need to restructure an organisation but there was no strategic business plan to help with direction and implementation.

There was no formal input of strategic planning knowledge for the ARG members, apart from what they had acquired in their postgraduate management studies. However, they were familiar with the use of Action Learning Projects and understood the AR method used for the planning and implementation of change. This enabled the ARG and the CDTs to develop the strategic business plan and implement the restructuring process using the AR method. The performance outcomes results were achieved by the development of the strategic business plan, implementation of the restructuring process using the AR method.

The learning outcomes included the modification of norms to allow senior managers in the CDTs to participate in the discussions and decision making process, even though adherence to the Melanesian culture requires listening to elders as a sign of respect and acceptance of their decisions.

ARG and CDT members learnt to work in groups, learning to resolve problems in teams and developing plans, and problem-solving and decision making techniques.

The cyclical process of Action Research was used by the CEO, members of the ARG and the CDT as they worked together in planning, implementing the plans, observing, evaluating the progress and reflecting on the outcomes. They then repeated the cycle of planning, acting, observing and reflecting at each stage of establishing the strategic business plan and implementing the restructuring process through the AR process and cycles.

REFERENCES

Kincaide, G. 1997, "Building a New Organisational Framework", *Association Management* (November 1997), pp 35-41.

CHAPTER 5
EVALUATION OF A MANAGEMENT DEVELOPMENT PROGRAM
FOR AN ABORIGINAL COMMUNITY ORGANISATION

ABSTRACT

This chapter describes the methods used to evaluate a board management development program which was conducted for the Board members of Kuju CDEP Inc, an Aboriginal community organisation in Port Lincoln, South Australia.

CDEP is an acronym for Community Development and Employment Program, an Australian Government initiative to provide employment and training within Aboriginal communities.

This Work-Applied Board Management Development Program (BMDP) used the Action Research approach. It was carried out over fourteen months and comprised two stages, each involving the action research cycles of planning, action, observation, reflection and evaluation.

INTRODUCTION

In this evaluation of the BMDP, data collected by participant observation of the development of the Board members was evaluated using triangulation involving the facilitator, the Board members, other staff of the organisation, representatives of funding agencies, and representatives of the Department of Employment Education and Training (DEET) and the Department of Technical and Further Education (DETAFE).

Content analysis was carried out on the evaluation reports, the recorded observations of the facilitator and a video recording of the Final Evaluation Workshop. Data from this content analysis was analysed for significant differences using the chi-square and Fisher tests.

The evaluation of Board members in the BMDP was based on the recommendations of reports (1985 and 1989) that training programs for Aboriginal community leaders should aim to improve confidence and self-esteem, commitment and a range of management skills and knowledge.

This view was in keeping with the ideas of Kirkpatrick (cited in Yorks 2005), who stressed evaluation of the trainees' reaction to the program, learning by the trainees, behavioural changes by the trainees and results in terms of organisational performance, and those of Parker (1973) who emphasised the evaluation of individual job performance, group performance, trainee satisfaction and trainee knowledge gained. The Kirkpatrick model of evaluation has been further extended by Phillips (cited in Yorks 2005) to include return on investment as a fifth level of evaluation.

The evaluation in this BMDP focused on the development of the Board members as a group and their perceived increases in understanding and application of management skills and knowledge, increases in confidence and self-esteem and increases in commitment. The evaluation did not focus on individual Board members since the facilitator's contract for the design and implementation of the BMDP specified the development of the Board as a group and the Board members specifically requested that individual evaluations should not be carried out.

A naturalistic, qualitative, goal-free evaluation approach was adopted, as suggested by Bramley (1991) and Easterby-Smith 1986, 1994). The techniques of triangulation, as recommended by Burgess (1984), Elliott (1976-77) and Forward (1989), and critical self-reflection, as suggested by Argyris, Putnam and McLain Smith (1985) and Kemmis and McTaggart (1988) were used.

Data for the triangulations were obtained by participant observation and the use of self-reports in addition to data collected from other independent observers.

Statistical analysis of the three development variables, namely, confidence, commitment and management skills and knowledge, was carried out by testing if there was a difference in the proportion of positive and negative comments before and after the program.

A null hypothesis of no change and an alternative hypothesis of a perceived improvement were tested. Each variable could be represented in a 2 x 2 contingency table as shown in Table 5.1.

Table 5.1 – Confidence

	+	-
BEFORE	0.0	4.3
AFTER	20.7	0

However, this is not a typical related pairs analysis and the data were treated as two separate groups of observations. The terms 'before' and 'after' are used for convenience, not in their technical sense.

The relevant treatment here (Levin 1981) is to use the chi-square statistical test when all expected frequencies based on the null hypothesis are greater than or equal to five. When any expected frequency falls below five the Fisher exact probability test (Siegel 1956; Sprent 1989) is used. In all cases, the analysis was carried out on raw frequencies although percentages are used in the tables for cross-comparison purposes.

To provide an insight into the types of comments that were made and to demonstrate that these statements do help to establish the development of the Board members, a qualitative, descriptive analysis of the data is first presented considering in turn, each of the areas of confidence and self-esteem, commitment and management skills and knowledge. This is followed by the results of a quantitative content analysis of the data to confirm the conclusions from the qualitative analysis.

QUALITATIVE ANALYSIS OF BOARD MEMBERS AS A GROUP

Data triangulation was carried out using comments made by the evaluators, the Board members and the facilitator. The evaluators included the Kuju CDEP Administrator, three representatives from the funding agency Aboriginal & Torres Strait Islanders Corporation (ATSIC), three representatives from the Technical and Further Education (TAFE) School of Aboriginal Administration including the TAFE Community Management Trainer, a Department of Education Employment and Training (DEET)/Aboriginal Education Employment Development Unit (AEEDU) representative, staff members of Kuju CDEP and new Board members.

Data triangulation was achieved by using multiple sources of data as follows:

1. The written reports submitted at the First and Final Evaluation Workshops;
2. The videotape recording of the Final Evaluation Workshop; and
3. The observations of the facilitator as recorded in his notes made during the program.

Comments made by the evaluators, Board members and the facilitator are presented below under the headings of confidence and self-esteem, commitment, and the understanding and application of management skills and knowledge.

Confidence and Self Esteem

The Regional Manager of ATSIC, commenting on the Board members' development following Stage I, wrote:

> I was impressed with the confidence displayed by the participants in their presentations, especially those people who were new to the course.

The observations of the facilitator (recorded in his notes) support the idea of the growth in confidence and self-esteem of the Board. The facilitator also noted the confident manner with which the Board members were able to answer questions and themselves ask questions of the evaluators at the Final Evaluation Workshop and the increased confidence which was displayed when they presented their strategic plan at the Kuju CEDP AGM.

Staff members and the new Board members also commented on improvements in self-esteem and confidence, particularly in public speaking. For example:

> Members were transformed from "head down don't look at me people" to assertive well spoken members of a working Board (a new Board Member).

> With the Board members having the opportunity of doing the Board Management Development Program, I feel it has benefited the whole Board in public speaking and feeling confident in themselves (a new Board member).

> The Board members' personal growth has really shown. When I speak to them they are so confident, their shyness is not there (a new Board Member).

The TAFE Community Management Trainer suggested that "a lot of the success of the Kuju Board members stems from their increased self-confidence and self-esteem" while an ATSIC representative stressed the increased confidence of the Board as a group:

> The project exudes a feeling of confidence in dealing with local issues. There is a newfound confidence born out of the knowledge that as a Board there is unity and consensus agreement about the issues. The DEET/AEEDU representative commented, "The confidence and public speaking factor stands out very clearly".

Increased confidence and self-esteem were mentioned frequently during the Final Evaluation Workshop. The ATSIC representative stated that this was where she had observed the most growth:

> When you first started I saw a number of fairly shy people lacking in confidence and that's one of the things that I have seen that's grown the most.

> People are willing to speak up when the need arises.

Another TAFE representative, himself an Aboriginal, in reference to the Board, said:

> You have become a reasonably powerful group. People will listen to you. That gives us Aboriginal people in South Australia status, and that's very important. When you talk to people, you talk with authority.

The Board Chairperson, in a jointly prepared report with the Administrator, described how confidence and self-esteem had been built up. They stated that:

> Nearing the end of the BMDP, Board members were encouraged to participate in presentations using overhead projectors. This was a major step in developing confidence and although the presentations were not long, showed the progress Board members had made. Before the BMDP, some of those who had not even spoke in Board Meetings except the raising of a hand or a yes or a no began to speak and discuss.

> It is important to note that the Board was given encouragement as they progressed. It was continually pointed out to them the things they had achieved and how much they were progressing. Now the loudest did not always get their own way as the Board members began to gain confidence and self-esteem.

These various comments indicate that the Board members were perceived to have increased in confidence and self-esteem.

Commitment
The Administrator, in his summary report following Stage 1 of the BMDP, noted:

> The attendance for the Issues Modules has also been excellent with members eager to learn. It should be noted that Kuju CDEP Board members receive no additional pay or monetary incentive to undertake this program.
>
> This, I believe, shows the commitment of these people to the program.

Commitment was also observed by the facilitator during the program. He noted that the Board members were strongly committed to the BMDP and in particular to the development of the strategic plan for Kuju CDEP. This was shown by their attendance, their willingness to sacrifice personal commitments to attend sessions and their high level of involvement in developing the plan.

The Administrator painted a grim picture of the early days of Kuju CDEP in his report. Board members had lacked skills and experience, many having a long history of unemployment. The Board had little management expertise and there were few policies or guidelines for the running of the programs. Conflict at meetings had resulted in poor attendance and the Board had not functioned effectively.

He noted improvement in a number of areas by the Board members and suggested that they had developed during the program.

> Some Board members were irregular in their attendance. Strategies were introduced through Action Orientated Learning and Problem Solving. Participants of the training program were teamed up and were responsible for seeing their partners knew the training was on and turned up.
>
> The effects of this training program have been excellent. The Board has come to an understanding of real management and their responsibilities.

He also listed "commitment" of the Board as one of the programs' strengths.

In a report, written jointly by the Chairperson and the Administrator, commitment before the program was contrasted with the commitment since the program began:

> There were a few Board members that would attend Meetings regularly. However, the majority would attend irregularly.

This made it very difficult to gain Board approval. When there was conflict within the community concerning an issue to Kuju Board, members would always avoid coming.

Quite often Board members would simply forget completely about the time set for Board meetings. Also other activities would be given priority over these Board meetings such as:

- Shopping
- Drinking
- Playing cards
- Family activities
- Funerals
- Sport

The weather would also influence the attendance of meetings and also the day would affect the attendance such as: if it was a Friday, a day after pay day, attendance would be down.

Attendance or commitment during the overall BMDP was around 90%. This occurred because of:

- The facilitator making plain the high expectations for those who were involved.

- The Board being made to realise the cost of this program and that it was the first and a very special program.

- The buddy system, teaming up Board members ensuring that 1 member at least had transport. Pointing out that everyone in that team was responsible for reminding and picking up the other person.

The above strategies worked well, and this was shown by the regular and high attendance for this program. This also established good habits and commitment for the attendance of Board meetings.

In the TAFE Community Management Trainer's report, he contrasted the early days of Kuju CDEP, when "the Board seemed to be in a state of continual crisis" with problems stemming from the inexperience of the Board members, personality conflicts and poor attendance at meetings, with the present situation:

> The first thing they learned was that if you are going to learn you have to be prepared to turn up at training sessions. At that time, attendance at Meetings organised by Kuju was not good. Your Board members have really shown that they can apply themselves and succeed. I think the reason for this is that the course made you realise that what you were doing was worthwhile and that you really could succeed.

Individual Board members also recognised their increased commitment, for example, a Board member said:

> With the BMD program in the last twelve months commitment with the old Board members, attendance with the old Board members was very good, I feel that is a strength.

> I must admit in the last few months we have had a lack of commitment and attendance, with the new Board members since they were selected.

An ATSIC representative also referred to commitment in his report:

> One of the outstanding and critical features of success of the BMDP is that it requires a high level of commitment from participants. This has been clearly evident as most Board members have completed at least a good proportion of the course.

The initial problems of motivation and attendance were mentioned by several Board members and the "buddy system" that was devised to overcome this problem was described. One of the Board members stated that "it's very hard for an Aboriginal to keep an appointment on his own". Another ATSIC representative commented:

> There's motivation there now and I think that there was motivation before but people didn't know how to handle it. You have been given a structure and you are working that out for yourselves.

These various comments indicate that the Board members were perceived to have increased in commitment.

The Understanding and Application of Management Skills and Knowledge
The need for management training was recognised by the ATSIC representative. He wrote: "The most important issue which Kuju needs to resolve at the present time is the establishment of a strong Board of Management".

Evidence of development of management skills and knowledge is provided by the written output from the BMDP, including the problem solving exercises, the strengths and weaknesses of Kuju CEDP programs and the Kuju CDEP strategic plan.

The ATSIC representative's report described the untenable situation in which the Board was attempting to operate before the BMDP. An unskilled and inexperienced management group, divided by factional interests and lacking clear purpose and direction, was making ad hoc decisions and stumbling from one crisis to the next. He noted that "there was a real concern that the whole operation could fold".

That there has been an improvement in the operation of the Board is supported by his statement that "in dealings with the Central Office, Canberra, Kuju is mentioned as exemplary in its operations". He pointed to increased communication skills of individual members, better communication between staff, Board members and participants, a decrease in the need for outside assistance, and a unity of direction with all Board members contributing to the decision making process.

The ATSIC representative also noted that "the language and understanding of management principles is evident in oral and written presentations" and he stressed the value of a strategic planning document prepared by the Board members "which clearly outlines the organisation mission, medium term goals and the strategies devised to attain these goals" and suggested that "it is evident from these changes that not only do Board members know more about the principles of management, but they are also experiencing the application of this learning". In a summary section he wrote:

> In evaluating the objectives of the BMDP against outcomes it is quite clear that the program is effectively meeting its objectives. It is often the case that there is no physical evidence of this but the climate of the project exudes confidence and organisation. Certainly in terms of capital growth Kuju boasts an impressive asset inventory mainly attributed to the efficiency and effectiveness of its operations.

Improvements in decision-making and problem-solving skills, planning and involvement were observed and recorded by staff members. One staff member said:

> Since the commencement of the Board Management Training Course, I have seen change and growth in all Board members understanding modern day management.
>
> The Board has been instrumental in implementing new policies for a guideline to work with. The Board feels that their training has been instrumental in the success of Kuju CDEP and have passed a Policy that all future intending Board members must agree to attend Board Training Programs.

An administrative staff member said:

> Matters regarding budgets and forward planning are no longer a foreign language to the Board. They are now in control of Kuju CDEP and the making of decisions has become second nature to them. Had it not been for the Board Management Training Program Kuju CDEP would still be muddling along with most decisions made by Administration staff and rubber stamped by the Board or, as is the case with some other schemes, entirely run by the Administration staff who are predominantly white.

This situation was contrasted by the Administrator with what happened at Board meetings during the program:

> The BMDP brought the Board of Kuju from unawareness to awareness to real Board management, and showed them how they were to be involved in putting this into practice. This was demonstrated at the Board meetings that were held during the period of this program. Everyone started to attend Board meetings and when issues were raised everyone would put forward their thoughts and discuss them; then a decision was made. Board members were finally able to deal with the problems and issues. This was due to the Board Management Development Program on problem-solving and decision-making and a chart was drawn up to make these clear.
>
> Staff issues and participant issues of Kuju's employees began to be looked at instead of being avoided. By the end of the BMDP a Mission Statement had been produced with goals and strategies for the next three years. Knowledge was being applied.

There were many comments made during the Final Evaluation Workshop about the improved management skills of the Board, including better communication, both within the Board and between the Board members and other Kuju CDEP participants. An interesting observation was made by the Administrator about the decision-making process, which in the early days was very much ad hoc and spur of the moment:

> The management, the thought processes, the problem solving, and decision making has put the brakes on everybody. The Board doesn't get pushed into making decisions.

The need for management training was described by a staff member of Kuju CDEP:

> We could see a need within our organisation that we need training of our participants on CDEP to have our Board trained to understand modern day management: the right procedures and how to manage. We just keep it as an on-going thing to train our participants and our Board members to have a better understanding of management which has been lacking in Aboriginal communities.

> People have been put on Boards and they're making decisions, but half the time they don't know the decision they're making; it could be the wrong decision. This training here gives them the skills to make the right decision. So they know about conflict management and managing; when to say "no" and when to say "yes", so they can deal with this fairly for the whole organisation.

> So that's been the main issue for the training program, for the Board to know modern day management and to understand that, when they're passing anything or bringing policies in and general control over the whole Kuju CDEP.

Improvement in conflict resolution procedures also featured in many of the comments, for example, a Board member noted:

> When the Board started off, when we used to have meetings, we never used to all agree on a certain subject. We were all arguing amongst ourselves at one another throats. But after we did this course, we found that we could sit down and discuss a matter in a civilised manner and at the end of the day, we walk out with the same decision, feeling good about it.

An ATSIC representative said:

> So it's that conflict resolution that you've been working
> through and those communications skills; taking
> opportunities out of those situations rather than seeing them
> as problems so much.

The application of this newly acquired knowledge to the management of
programs within Kuju CDEP was also highlighted.

A DEET/AEEDU representative stated that the Board now has "a
common vision and a common direction". He stressed the importance of
planning for organisations wishing to attract funding, citing Kuju as an
example of a program with a clear sense of direction:

> Kuju is continually mentioned interstate in our central
> office as being one of the most effective CDEP programs in
> the country and certainly one of the most progressive.

> You now have the skills to logically analyse any situation
> that's put in front of you so that the emotional issues don't
> get a chance to come out.

The increased understanding and the application of management
skills of Board members was also observed by the facilitator all through
the program.

From a qualitative analysis of the available data, this section has
provided evidence that there has been a perceived increase in confidence
and self-esteem, commitment and the understanding and application
of management skills and knowledge among the Board members
as a group. In the next section, a quantitative content analysis of the
data is presented.

QUANTITATIVE ANALYSIS OF BOARD MEMBERS AS A GROUP

Content analysis was carried out on the evaluation reports, the recorded
observations of the facilitator and the videotape recording of the Final
Evaluation Workshop.

Opinionated statements were placed in categories according to whether
they referred to the Board members before or after the program, whether
the statement was positive or negative, and whether the statement referred
to the understanding and the application of management skills and
knowledge, commitment or confidence and self-esteem.

In the following section, the analysis of the opinions of the evaluators,
the Board members and the facilitator are first presented individually and
then brought together for data triangulation.

Content Analysis of Opinions made by the Evaluators
A question asked in the BMDP program was:

Did the evaluators perceive the Board members as a group to have increased in:

- confidence and self-esteem;
- commitment; and
- the understanding and application of management skills and knowledge?

This section answers this question. Table 5.2 shows the improvement in confidence, self-esteem and public speaking of the Board members, as perceived by the evaluators. There were no positive comments about the Board members before the BMDP on any of these areas and no negative comments referring to the Board members after the BMDP. The number of positive comments referring to confidence and public speaking after the program was high and there were a number of negative statements referring to confidence and public speaking before the program.

The differences among the results for "Commitment" in Table 5.2 are smaller, but these results also show a trend with more positive than negative comments referring to after (or during) the BMDP and more negative statements than positive referring to before the BMDP.

In the analysis of these data, the number of statements in each category was expressed as a percentage of the total number of statements. Since each percentage was rounded to one decimal place, the total of the individual percentages is not exactly 100.

The list of categories in Table 5.2 under the 'Management Skills and Knowledge' heading includes those characteristics that a management training and development program might be expected to have improved in trainees. According to the statements made by the evaluators, there had been an improvement in most of these and it is worth noting that even though there were no references (positive or negative) to counselling, it does not necessarily mean that this did not also improve, only that it was not highlighted during the evaluation.

The most frequently mentioned areas of improvement were goal-setting, planning, problem-solving, decision-making, conflict resolution and communication. The 'Management (general)' category included comments that did not refer to any particular skill or knowledge area.

For increased clarity, this matrix was reduced using 'pragmatic' reduction, which is described by Carney (1972 p. 227) as "separating an array of cells into a smaller number of 'types,' each comprising a combination of cells." Krippendorf (1980) referred to this as 'clustering'.

Table 5.2 – Content Analysis of the Opinions of the Evaluators

CONFIDENCE & SELF-ESTEEM	FREQUENCY PERCENTAGES			
	BEFORE BMDP		AFTER BMDP	
	+	-	+	-
Confidence	0	2.1	11.1	0
Self-esteem	0	1.1	2.1	0
Public Speaking	0	0	6.4	0
Independence	0	1.1	1.1	0
Totals	**0**	**4.3**	**20.7**	**0**
COMMITMENT				
Involvement	0	0	0.5	0
Attendance	0.5	2.1	2.1	0
Strength	0	0	0	0
Commitment	0.5	1.6	2.1	0
Totals	**1.0**	**3.7**	**4.7**	**0**
MANAGEMENT SKILL & KNOWLEDGE				
Goal setting	0	1.6	5.3	0
Planning	0	0.5	4.3	0
Organising	0	1.1	1.1	0
Leadership	0	0	0.5	0
Problem solving	0	0	3.2	0
Application of knowledge	0	0	2.7	0
Conflict resolution	0	3.2	3.2	0
Decision making	0	2.1	5.9	0
Group cohesiveness	0	0.5	2.1	0
Counselling	0	0	0	0
Meeting procedure	0	0.5	1.6	0
Time management	0	0.5	0	0
Communication	0	0.5	3.7	0
Budgeting	0	0	0.5	0
Policy-making	0	0.5	2.7	0
Effectiveness of Board	0	1.1	2.7	0
Sharing of knowledge	0	0	1.1	0
Management experience	0.5	2.7	0	0.5
Evaluation	0	0.5	0.5	0
Management (general)	0	2.7	5.5	0
Totals	**0.5**	**18**	**46.6**	**0.5**

Table 5.3 is the result of clustering the data from Table 5.2 into the major categories of Confidence and Self-Esteem, Commitment and Management Skills and Knowledge. Raw frequencies are included in brackets after each frequency percentage.

This reduced matrix shows more clearly the perceived changes in the confidence and self-esteem, commitment and management skills and knowledge of the Board Members. The data in this table were then analysed to see if the observed differences were statistically significant.

Table 5.3 – Content Analysis of the Opinions of the Evaluators – Clustering Matrix

	FREQUENCY PERCENTAGE			
	BEFORE BMDP %		**AFTER BMDP %**	
	+	**-**	**+**	**-**
Confidence & Self-Esteem	0(0)	S4.3(8)	20.7(39)	0(0)
Commitment	1.0(2)	3.7(7)	4.7(9)	0(0)
Management Skill and Knowledge	0.5(1)	18.0(34)	46.6(91)	0.5(1)

Statistical Analysis of Data
Calculations were made on the raw data set of 192. P values, calculated for one degree of freedom, were as follows:

1. Confidence and Self-Esteem $\quad$ P < 0.001
2. Commitment $\quad$ P < 0.001
3. Management skills and knowledge $\quad$ P < 0.001

These values disconfirm the null hypothesis and provide support for the alternative hypothesis that the evaluators perceived that the Board members as a group have increased:

- in confidence and self-esteem;
- in commitment; and
- in the understanding and application of management skills and knowledge.

Content Analysis of Opinions made by the Board Members
Another question asked in the BMDP was:

Did the indigenous community leaders as a group perceive themselves as having increased in:

- confidence and self-esteem;
- commitment; and
- the understanding and application of management skills and knowledge?

This section answers this question. Table 5.4 shows the improvement in confidence, self-esteem and public speaking of the Board members, as perceived by themselves. There were no positive comments about the Board members as a group before the BMDP on any of these areas and no negative comments referring to the Board members after the BMDP.

There were, however, several positive comments referring to confidence, self-esteem and public speaking after the program and one negative comment referring to public speaking before the program.

A similar trend can be seen in the area of commitment where there were no positive comments on involvement, attendance, strength or commitment referring to the Board members before the BMDP but several referring to these areas after the BMDP. There were twice as many negative comments referring to commitment before the BMDP as negative comments referring to commitment after the BMDP.

In the management skills and knowledge category, the main improvements highlighted by the Board members were in planning, problem solving, application of knowledge, conflict resolution, decision making, effectiveness of the Board and general management. There were no positive comments on any area before the BMDP and no negative comments referring to the Board members after the BMDP.

Table 5.4 – Content Analysis of the Opinions of the Board Members

CONFIDENCE & SELF-ESTEEM	FREQUENCY PERCENTAGE			
	BEFORE BMDP		AFTER BMDP	
	+	-	+	-
Confidence	0	0	4.1	0
Self-esteem	0	0	4.1	0
Public speaking	0	2.0	2.0	0
Independence	0	0	0	0
Totals	**0**	**2.0**	**10.2**	**0**
COMMITMENT				
Involvement	0	0	0	0
Attendance	0	0	2.0	2.0
Strength	0	0	2.0	0
Commitment	0	8.2	8.2	2.0
Totals	**0**	**8.2**	**12.2**	**4.0**
MANAGEMENT SKILLS & KNOWLEDGE				
Goal setting	0	0	0	0
Planning	0	0	8.2	0
Organising	0	0	2.0	0
Leadership	0	0	0	0
Problem solving	0	2.0	6.1	0
Application of knowledge	0	0	4.1	0
Conflict resolution	0	2.0	8.2	0
Decision making	0	0	10.2	0
Group cohesiveness	0	0	2.0	0
Counselling	0	0	0	0
Meeting procedure	0	0	0	0
Time management	0	0	0	0
Communication	0	2.0	0	0
Budgeting	0	0	0	0
Policy-making	0	0	2.0	0
Effectiveness of Board	0	0	6.1	0
Sharing of knowledge	0	0	2.0	0
Management experience	0	0	0	0
Evaluation	0	0	0	0
Management (general)	0	0	6.1	0
Totals	**0**	**6.0**	**57.0**	**0**

Table 5.5 is the result of clustering the data from Table 5.4 into the major categories of Confidence and Self-Esteem, Commitment and Management Skills and Knowledge.

This reduced matrix shows more clearly the perceived changes in the confidence and self-esteem,commitment and management skills and knowledge of the Board Members. The data in this table were then analysed to see if the observed differences were statistically significant.

Table 5.5 – Content Analysis of the Opinions of the Board Members – Clustering Matrix

	FREQUENCY PERCENTAGE			
	BEFORE BMDP		AFTER BMDP	
	+	-	+	-
Confidence & Self-Esteem	0(0)	2.0(1)	10.2(5)	0(0)
Commitment	0(0)	8.2(4)	12.2(6)	4.0(2)
Management Skill and Knowledge	0(0)	6.0(3)	57.0(28)	0(0)

Statistical Analysis of Data

Calculations were done on the raw data set of 49. P values calculated for one degree of freedom were as follows:

  1. Confidence and Self-Esteem   P = 0.166
  2. Commitment   P = 0.03
  3. Management Skills and Knowledge   P = 0.00003

The values for commitment and management skills and knowledge disconfirm the null hypothesis and provide support for the alternative hypothesis that the Board members perceived themselves as a group to have increased in commitment and the understanding and application of management skills and knowledge.

The higher P value for confidence and self-esteem can be explained by the low total number of comments in this area. It is important to note that the data on confidence, while not providing strong support for the hypothesis of perceived improvement, do not disconfirm this hypothesis.

Table 5.6 – Content Analysis of Participant Observation by the Facilitator

CONFIDENCE & SELF-ESTEEM	FREQUENCY PERCENTAGE			
	BEFORE BMDP		AFTER BMDP	
	+	-	+	-
Confidence	0	1.2	15.1	1.8
Self-esteem	0	0.6	3.6	0
Public speaking	0	0	0.6	0
Independence	0	0	0	0
Totals	**0**	**1.8**	**19.3**	**1.8**
COMMITMENT				
Involvement	0	0	0.6	0.6
Attendance	0	0	1.8	1.2
Strength	0	1.2	0	0
Commitment	0	0.6	8.4	0.6
Totals	**0**	**1.8**	**10.8**	**2.4**
MANAGEMENT SKILLS & KNOWLEDGE				
Goal setting	0	1.8	3.6	0
Planning	0	4.2	8.4	0
Organising	0	0.6	1.2	0
Leadership	0	0.6	1.2	0
Problem solving	0	0	8.4	0
Application of knowledge	0	0	6.0	0
Conflict resolution	0	0	3.0	0
Decision making	0	0.6	3.0	0
Group cohesiveness	0	0	1.8	0
Counselling	0	0	0	0
Meeting procedure	0	0.6	0	0
Time management	0	0	1.2	0
Communication	0	0	1.8	0
Budgeting	0	0	0	0
Policy-making	0	1.8	0	0
Effectiveness of Board	0	0.6	1.2	0
Sharing of knowledge	0	0	0	0
Management experience	0	0.6	0	0
Evaluation	0	0.6	3.6	0
Management (general)	0	1.2	4.2	0
Totals	**0**	**13.2**	**48.6**	**0**

Content Analysis of Facilitator's Observations
Another question asked in this BMDP was:

Did the facilitator perceive the Board members as a group to have increased in:

- confidence and self-esteem;
- commitment; and
- the understanding and application of management skills and knowledge?

This section answers this question.

The analysis of the facilitator's participant observations (Table 5.6) during the program shows a similar trend to the other content analyses. Again, confidence improvement was highlighted, but there was a smaller emphasis on public speaking.

The commitment of the Board was mentioned more frequently. Within the area of management skills and knowledge, planning, problem-solving, and decision-making were again highlighted. In addition, goal setting, application of knowledge and evaluation were also emphasised.

Table 5.7 is the result of clustering the data from Table 5.6 into the major categories of Confidence and Self-esteem, Commitment and Management Skills and Knowledge. This reduced matrix shows more clearly the perceived changes in the confidence and self-esteem, commitment, and management skills and knowledge of the Board Members. The data in this table were then analysed to see if the observed differences were statistically significant.

Table 5.7 – Content Analysis of Participant Observation by the Facilitator – Clustering Matrix

	FREQUENCY PERCENTAGE			
	BEFORE BMDP%		AFTER BMDP %	
	+	-	+	-
Confidence & Self-esteem	0(0)	1.8(3)	19.3(32)	1.8(3)
Commitment	0(0)	1.8(3)	10.8(18)	2.4(4)
Management Skill and Knowledge	0(0)	13.2(22)	48.6(81)	0(0)

Statistical Analysis of Data

Calculations were done on the raw data set of 166. P values, calculated for one degree of freedom, were as follows:

1) Confidence and Self-Esteem	$P = 0.002$
2) Commitment	$P = 0.015$
3) Management Skills and Knowledge	$P < 0.001$

These values disconfirm the null hypothesis and provide support for the alternative hypothesis that the facilitator perceived the Board members as a group to have increased in confidence and self-esteem, commitment, and the understanding and application of management of skills and knowledge.

DATA TRIANGULATION

The data from these three sources, the evaluators, the Board members and the facilitator were then triangulated. The perceptions of the evaluators (the Administrator, the new Board members, funding agency representatives, the TAFE representatives, the DEET/AEEDU representative and other staff members) of the development of the Board members as a group were triangulated against the perceptions of the Board members of their own development as a group and the facilitator's perceptions of the Board members' development as a group.

Figures 5.1, 5.2 and 5.3 are bar graphs which bring all these data together for comparison, showing this triangulation. These graphs show that the observations of the facilitator are strongly supported by the observations of the evaluators and the opinions of the Board members themselves. They also demonstrate the following trends:

i) There has been a perceived improvement in the confidence and self-esteem of the Board members as a group as a result of their participation in the BMDP (Figure 5.1);
ii) There has been a perceived increase in the commitment of the Board members as a group as a result of their participation in the BMDP (Figure 5.2); and
iii) There has been a perceived increase in the understanding of the application of management skills and knowledge of the Board members as a group as a result of their participation in the BMDP (Figure 5.3).

A comparison of the three graphs shows that by far the greatest number of statements were made about management skills and knowledge, followed by confidence, with commitment scoring the least.

Figure 5.1 – Confidence and Self-esteem of the Board Members as a Group

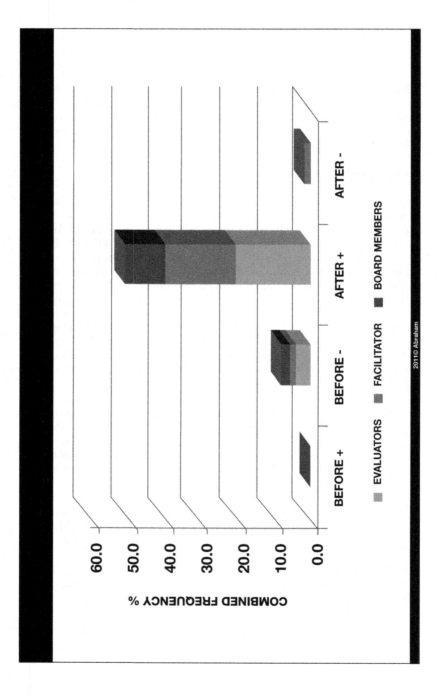

Figure 5.2 – Commitment of the Board Members as a Group

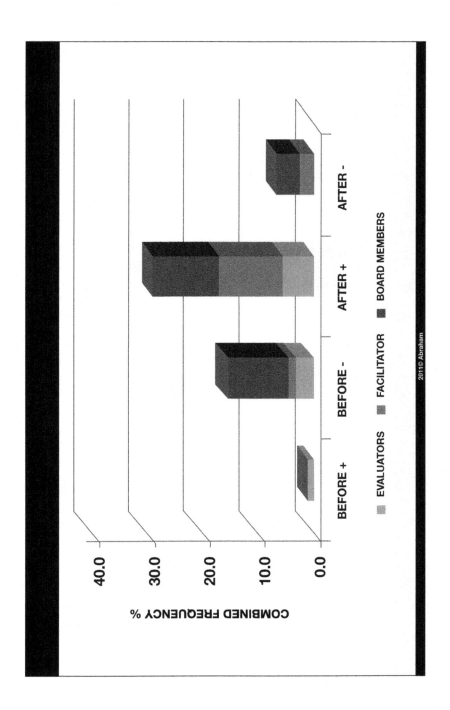

Figure 5.3 – Understanding of application of Management Skills and Knowledge of the Board members as a Group

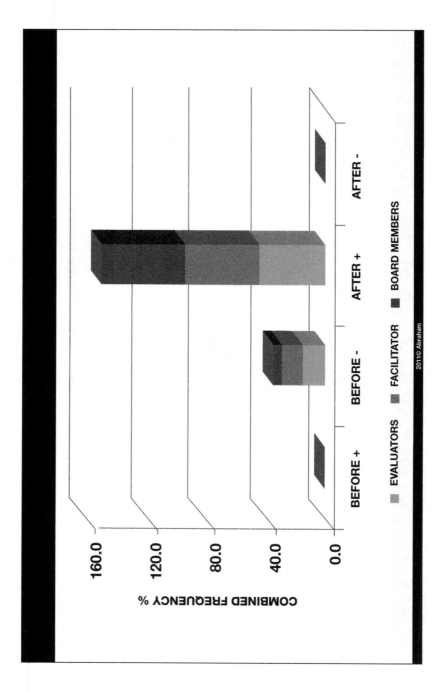

The Board's development as a group was further evidenced by the document that the Board had prepared and presented to the Kuju CDEP Annual General Meeting (AGM), which included an analysis of Kuju CDEP's programs and the strategic plan.

An examination of the qualitative analysis and the quantitative content analysis shows a similar trend in the perceived increased confidence and self-esteem, commitment, and the understanding and application of management skills and knowledge of the Board members as a group.

CONCLUSION

In this study, the results of the evaluation of the development as a group of the Kuju CDEP Board members who attended the Board Management Development Program were presented. The formal evaluation of the Board members occurred during evaluation workshops held at the end of Stages I and II.

The Board members' development was evaluated using data triangulation. One set of data comprised the reports of the evaluators and the Board members as well as the facilitators' notes.

This data was then triangulated against the the perceptions of the following parties of how the Board members as a group had developed as a result of the BMDP:

- the evaluators;
- the Board members themselves; and
- the facilitator.

The data analysis showed that the Board members were perceived to have increased in confidence and self-esteem, in commitment, and in the understanding and application of management skills and knowledge.

Statements made referring to the Board members as a group, in the evaluation reports during the Final Evaluation Workshop and in the facilitator's notes, support these findings.

REFERENCES

A Chance for the Future: Training in Skills for Aboriginal and Torres Strait Island Community Management and Development 1989, the report of the House of Representatives Standing Committee on Aboriginal Affairs.

Argyris, C, Putnam, R, & McLain Smith, D 1985, *Action Science*, Jossey-Bass, San Francisco.

Bramley, P 1991, *Evaluating Training Effectiveness: Translating Theory*, McGraw Hill, London.

Burgess, R G 1984, *In the Field: An Introduction to Field Research*, George Allen and Unwin Ltd, London.

Carney, T F 1972, *Content Analysis: .A Technique for Systematic Inference from Communications*, Winnipeg, Canada: University of Manitoba Press.

Easterby-Smith, M 1986, *Evaluation of Management Education, Training and Development*, Gower Publishing Company Ltd., Aldershot, Hants., England.

Easterby-Smith, M 1994, Evaluating Management Development, Training and Education, Gower Publishing Company, Aldershot.

Elliot, J 1976-1977, 'Developing hypotheses about classrooms from teachers' practical constructs: An account of the work of the Ford Teaching Project', in Kemmis, S & McTaggart, R (Eds.) 1988, *The Action Research Reader*, 3rd ed., Deakin University Press, Melbourne, 121-122.

Forward, D 1989, 'A Guide to Action Research', in Lomax, P (Ed.), *The Management of Change: Increasing School Effectiveness and Facilitating Staff Development Through Action Research*, Multilingual Matters Ltd., Clevedon, Philadelphia, 29-39.

Kemmis, S & McTaggart, R 1988, *The Action Research Planner*, 3rd ed. Deakin University Press, Melbourne.

Krippendorff, K 1980, *Content Analysis: An Introduction to its Methodology*, California: Sage Publications Inc.

Levin, R I 1987, *Statistics for Management*, 2nd ed., Prentice-Hall Englewood Cliffs, New Jersey.

Parker, T C 1973, 'Evaluation: The Forgotten Finale of Training', *Personnel*, AMACOM, New York, 50, 6, 61-63.

Report of the Committee of Review of Aboriginal Employment and Training Programmes, *(The Miller Report)*, 1985, Commonwealth Government of Australia.

Siegel, S 1956, *Non Parametric Statistics for the Behavioural Sciences*, McGraw-Hill, NewYork.

Sprent, P 1989, *Applied Non Parametric Statistical Methods*, 2nd ed., Chapman and Hall, London/New York.

Yorks L 2005, *Strategic Human Resource Development in Organizations*, South-Western College Publishing, Mason, Ohio.

CHAPTER 6
A GLOBAL CENTRE FOR WORK-APPLIED LEARNING AND RESEARCH
Dennis Hardy

ABSTRACT

In the first chapter, the concept and practice of Work-Applied Learning was introduced, providing the foundation on which the rest of the book rests. Thus, the next three chapters presented case studies of Work-Applied Learning in contrasting circumstances, demonstrating its versatility and robust nature. These were, in turn, followed by a chapter to show, in relation to a practical example, the importance of evaluation.

In this penultimate chapter, we move into the arena of education and research. We look first at how the Australian Institute of Business (AIB) has evolved as a global centre for Work-Applied Learning, so that it now occupies a niche position in Australian and global higher education in business and management . In the second section, the focus is on research in the context of Work-Applied Learning, including the specialised work-applied programs offered by AIB.

THE PRACTICAL BUSINESS SCHOOL

This section tells of the evolution of a place of education, training, consultancy and research, built on a distinctive foundation of Work-Applied Learning principles.

As we learnt in the first chapter, our story starts more than a quarter of a century ago with the formation of a consultancy, Gibaran Management Consultants. In 1994, this consultancy which is now called the Australian Institute of Business (AIB) was approved by the Australian authorities as an awarding body and over time, the boundaries of this initial venture were progressively widened to encompass a broader remit of courses and research. Currently, coursework and research degree programs are being undertaken by students in various parts of the world including Singapore, Malaysia, Sri Lanka, Vietnam, United Kingdom, Ireland, Egypt, Trinidad & Tobago and Guyana.

AIB's strap-line is, appropriately, 'The Practical Business School', reflecting its grounding in the world of work. In pursuance of the goals of Work-Applied Learning, the vision and mission of the AIB are as follows:

To provide distinctive business and management education in national and international environments based on AIB's orientation towards Work-Applied Learning.

To provide access to quality, affordable and innovative work-applied business and management education, both locally and internationally, using the methods of Action Research and Action Learning (ARAL) and case research, thereby creating an environment for organizational and lifelong learning as well as supporting community and economic development.

AIB has a unique portfolio of courses and research programs. It is the only private business school in Australia which is accredited within the Australian Qualifications Framework to confer research degrees in business and management, namely, Master of Management (Research), Master of Management (Work-Based Learning), Doctor of Business Administration and Doctor of Philosophy. These are in addition to taught courses comprising the Bachelor of Business Administration and the Master of Business Administration, as well as a suite of vocational training programs.

(a) Embedding Work-Applied Learning

AIB systematically promotes and employs the Work-Applied Learning model throughout all aspects of its teaching and learning. This approach to the study of business and management makes AIB distinctive and forms the foundation of our academic content, delivery and assessment. The following are some of the ways in which this is achieved:

Workplace experience as entry requirement for students
The coursework and research programs include an entry requirement that candidates have workplace experience or access to a workplace. The purpose of this is to ensure that the student will have a familiar and accessible workplace context for the application of conceptual learning of the subjects. Indeed, a majority of students have completed their subjects contemporaneously with workplace employment, allowing them to apply learning in real-time as their studies proceed.

Selection of academic staff
The criteria for appointment of academic staff are:
- possession of an appropriate academic qualification from an accredited university or other institution of higher learning;
- appropriate working experience in the discipline/subject area in which the vacancy exists;

- relevant teaching experience at the appropriate level; and
- a commitment to the scholarship of teaching and learning.

'Appropriate academic qualifications' for academic staff would depend on the level of the course. For example, the minimum academic qualification to teach Master's level coursework would be a Master's degree, but preferably a DBA or PhD. In view of the work-applied nature of the courses, academic staff are required to have working experience in the discipline in which they teach, so that they can share with students real-life examples of scenarios in the workplace. Therefore, 'appropriate working experience' means at least three years' work experience at management level.

Training and development of academic facilitators
Notwithstanding the rigorous appointment criteria, all new academic staff are required to undergo a professional development programme. To assist with this, a Camtasia training package has been prepared and is issued to all postholders.

Design of courses and learning materials
Work-applied research is integrated in all of the AIB courses. Thus:

- Bachelor of Business Administration (BBA) students have to complete a two-subject, work-based research project under the supervision of a project supervisor, as well as undertaking a work-based assignment in every subject.
- Master of Business Administration (MBA) students have to complete a one-subject, work-based research project under the supervision of a project supervisor as well as a work-based assignment in every subject.
- Master of Management (Research) (MMgt) candidates in the Professional Pathway have to work on one or more research projects, equivalent to up to two thirds of the program; while those in the Research Pathway have to complete a work-applied research thesis.
- The Doctor of Business Administration (DBA) degree is a professional doctorate where candidates use the work-applied research methods of Case Research, Action Research or Reflective Practice to investigate business and management practices and policies. Research outcomes are presented in a 40,000 to 50,000 word thesis under the supervision of a Research Supervisor.
- Doctor of Philosophy (PhD) candidates are required to complete a thesis of between 60,000 and 80,000 words, under the supervision of a research supervisor, demonstrating the relationship of their research to the broader framework of the discipline or field of study. They will use the work-applied research methods of Case Research, Action Research or Reflective Practice.

Delivery approach

Subjects in taught courses normally include a work-based assignment or, in exceptional cases, one that is based on a case study. Ideally, the assignment should be of direct relevance and value to the student and their organisation (or an organisation of the student's choice). Such projects will be negotiated between student, workplace management and the facilitator in terms of scope, procedures and shared responsibilities.

Teaching/learning strategies used include:
- Action Learning groups;
- small group and one-to-one discussions;
- facilitator guided workplace projects;
- student sourced case studies; and
- case studies from the literature.

Course objectives are achieved as students integrate their readings, course materials and facilitator guidance into the workplace and through an iterative process of application and reflection.

Design of student assessments

At AIB, assessment responses are not intended to be merely a description of organisational procedures and practices, nor just an exposition of theory, but rather a combination of the two. The theory aspect should go beyond a summary or description and provide some critique or line of argument. That is, a balance must be achieved between theory and practice. In the pursuit of Work-Applied Management Learning, students must not overlook the practical application of conceptual and theoretical concepts. A pass mark will not be attained where there is no discussion of appropriate models, theories or concepts, nor will a student pass if his work fails to provide a cogent application of theory to actually work place scenarios.

(b) New Approaches to Work-Based Learning

New technologies are transforming the way we learn. The trend is away from traditional classrooms to online courses, collaborative ad hoc discussions, and easy access to information and subject specialists. At the same time, for private providers of higher degrees, the business aspects of education are becoming increasingly critical. Educators need to work more efficiently, make smarter, longer-lasting investments, and do more with less.

Learning and collaboration technologies, such as web conferencing, add live, real-time, multipoint interaction between researchers and enables dynamic, multi-way participation regardless of geographic location. Tools such as multipoint video, shared whiteboards and application sharing provide a research and learning environment that is as good, or in some aspects better, than traditional face-to-face classroom scenarios. Additionally, recording and publishing of interactions enable knowledge capture and review according to the students' own timelines and schedule. Web conferencing platforms facilitate instant, face-to-face communication and continuous collaboration between students, facilitators and research supervisors. This creates a form of learning that is accessible, personal, and meaningful. These benefits, however, do not come without their unique challenges, some of which are as follows:

For our educators:

- making education more active, effective, and personalised by addressing individual learning styles and special needs in the online environment;
- facilitating formal and informal learning, and meeting the needs of remote and mobile learners; and
- designing, delivering, and evolving high-quality teaching and research programs and measuring their efficacy.

For our administrators:

- ensuring that multiple facilitators and supervisors develop best practices, replicate consistent delivery, and ensure successful learning and research outcomes over time;
- making higher education more accessible and affordable for a global niche of business students and researchers, developing their contributions to policy and practice in the field of Work-Applied Management Learning;
- providing cost-effective professional development for faculty and staff ; and
- creating a culture of online collaboration across departments, campuses, research sites and between organisations.

For our students:

- dedicating themselves to this forward-looking model of distance learning, research and collaboration on a global scale and on-time, to achieve their learning and research outcomes;
- organising obligations of family and work to blend seamlessly with learning and research commitments, involving colleagues and supervisors widely dispersed across multiple time zones; and
- ensuring on-site computer hardware, software and connectivity resources are kept current, compatible and operational for the duration of the project.

At AIB we have set ourselves upon a course to meet these challenges and take a leading role in advancing online face-to-face collaborative teaching and research.

WORK-APPLIED RESEARCH

The former section has shown how AIB has evolved with a consistent orientation to different aspects of Work-Applied Learning. This section, in turn, will indicate the training and research components of the resultant portfolio.

AIB's distinctive research philosophy can be appreciated with reference to a series of steps: focus of research, the niche philosophy of research, its linkages to teaching and learning, and its staff. There is a strong focus on creativity, relationships between people and their society, and on bodies of knowledge. This is in line with the emphasis on 'creative work undertaken on a systematic basis in order to increase the stock of knowledge, including knowledge of man, culture, society, and the use of this stock of knowledge to devise new applications' (Australian Research Council, 2008).

In particular, AIB emphasises applied rather than basic research, that is, 'original investigation undertaken in order to acquire new knowledge but [is] directed primarily towards a specific, practical aim or objective' (Australian Research Council 2008).

The essential characteristic of this research activity is that it is not mere opinion (like that in talk-back radio or letters to a newspaper editor) but an approach that leads to argued positions based on carefully collected and analysed evidence that can be published through a peer review process.

Much research at AIB fits a niche area of work that is inductive rather than deductive. This niche concentration arises from its work-applied foundations. Much of the published research from business schools is of an abstract nature or presupposes a high level of quantitative analysis; as a result, it is not widely read by managers. Thus:

> *Most of the research is highly quantitative, hypothesis-driven and esoteric. As a result, it is almost universally unread by real-world managers (The Economist 2007).*

While most research in business schools is of this type, a much smaller proportion is qualitative (in less than one-quarter of articles, according to Hanson & Grimmer 2007). It is within this narrow field that AIB starts to be positioned.

AIB's research is similar in approach to that of Professor Barwise of the London Business School, who argues that qualitative, theory-building research means something to managers (The Economist 2007):

> *His own investigating of which research is filtering through to the journals managers and consultants might actually read has convinced him that inductive research—study which*

seeks to proceed without preconceptions, preferring to observe organisational behaviour and then to draw conclusions on what it finds—is much more likely to be applied in the real world than any other kind. But, he says, most of what actually makes academic journals is theory-driven.

In other words, AIB usually does research within the realism paradigm or philosophy (Sobh & Perry 2006), aiming at analytic generalisation rather than statistical generalisation (Yin 1994). In more detail, AIB's research data emphasises meaning rather than measurement, and its most common methodologies are the niche ones of case research and Action Research for building theories about managers in their real-world workplace (Stokes & Perry 2007; Zuber-Skerritt & Perry 2002).

(a) Research culture

A niche research approach based on Work-Applied Learning allows AIB to appropriately integrate its research with its other activities. Thus, the main features of the research culture at AIB include:

- a strategic approach to building work-applied research capabilities;
- the Research Contribution Scheme;
- Gibaran Journal of Applied Management;
- scholarships for work-applied research;
- the appointment of a Dean, experienced in work-applied research;
- work-applied research skills development; and
- research output.

A strategic approach to building work-applied research capabilities

It can be seen that the following goals have been established by the AIB as part of its strategic approach to building research capability over time:

- increase the number of research staff to supervise research candidates and research fellows in work-applied research projects in business and education;
- establish collaborative centres of excellence in work-applied research with select international institutions of higher learning and associations;
- recruit and increase the number of high quality research higher degree candidates nationally and internationally, to undertake work-applied research in business and education;
- undertake collaborative research and consultancy in Work-Applied Learning with organisations and management consultancies;
- share with international researchers and the corporate community the findings, conclusions and contributions of Work-Applied Learning through the Gibaran Journal of Applied Management, other international refereed publications, and national and international seminars and conferences;

- develop the work-applied research skills of research fellows and other researchers; and
- strengthen the infrastructure for research within AIB.

The Research Contribution Scheme

The Research Contribution Scheme, which is a customised version of the research fellowship schemes at universities, is an example of AIB's commitment to research in the field of work-applied business and management.

Most university research fellowship schemes are funded by research funds which enables them to appoint research fellows who are based full-time at their university for the duration of the fellowship. As it is a private institute, AIB does not receive research funds and, thus, all research activities have been self-funded. Therefore, the Research Contribution Scheme has been designed to provide opportunities for work-applied research, using minimum funding whereby researchers who are currently working fulltime in organisations are able to work collaboratively with the AIB on work-applied research projects.

The objectives of the Research Contribution Scheme are to:

- substantially strengthen Gibaran's work-applied research output;
- increase Gibaran's pool of higher degree supervisors; and
- provide leadership and mentoring to inexperienced researchers.

Membership is by invitation only and preference is given to applicants who are able to make a significant contribution to literature and work-applied management practice and policy using Action Research or Case Research. Benefits available include access to the research facilities at AIB's campus in Adelaide, access to an online library, access to an online Student Forum moderated by AIB, a designated title and the right to claim affiliation with the AIB, an honorarium for each article published in a peer-reviewed journal which indicates affiliation with AIB, and a monetary award to be used to attend and present papers at conferences and seminars.

The Gibaran Journal of Applied Management

The Gibaran Journal of Applied Management (http://journal.aib.edu.au/index.php/gjam) is committed to the discovery and application of business and management theory, and investigating how it is applied in organisations and work places. In particular, the Journal publishes scholarly articles, case studies and case analyses that combine academic rigour with practical application.

The Journal has particular interest in the investigation of the use of an integrated Action Research and Action Learning (ARAL) method, and how it is applied in an organisational or workplace context in areas such as entrepreneurship, strategy, operations, leadership, organisational change, marketing, finance, organisational learning and human resource management.

As AIB is committed to the use of the ARAL model, the Journal is a vehicle to share with the community of researchers and corporate leaders the findings and conclusions of its research. This does not preclude the fact that the Journal will also have scholarly contributions from all over the world on their own findings, conclusions and cases of work-applied research.

The Journal has adopted a double-blind peer review process to ensure that articles published demonstrate academic rigour and a commitment to exploring the application of business and management theory in an organisational or workplace setting. Reviewers (selected from an internationally-based panel) carefully consider submissions to ensure the articles are high quality and fit the Journal's objectives. From the start of 2012, the Journal has moved from being an annual publication to bi-annual.

Scholarships for work-applied research

Although AIB does not enjoy public funding to support the provision of research degree scholarships, it has chosen to make a limited number of these on its own account. These are available to domestic and international candidates, for DBA or PhD.

Existing academic staff who are interested in undertaking research higher degree studies at AIB are encouraged to do so. According to the Academic Staff Incentive Scheme, they may be given incentives such as a substantial discount of their course fees and paid study leave to be taken at a time that does not conflict with their normal duties.

A Dean experienced in work-applied research

In June 2011, I was appointed to the new position of Dean to lead the academic and research development of AIB. I started my career as an urban planner working in local government, before moving to higher education. I have extensive experience of research in a UK university, in both my own research activities and the management of others. With other academic and research staff at AIB, I am responsible for nurturing the culture of work-applied research at AIB.

Work-applied research skills development

Academic staff are encouraged to improve their research and publishing skills with the help of a dedicated staff development program. It includes the development of research supervision skills as well some of the mechanics of research plans and applications for research funding. There is also a focus on how to publish and present papers at conferences. Reflecting the priorities of AIB, the programme is based on the application of ARAL (Action Research and Action Learning).

Research Output
The output which signifies the research culture of AIB includes:

Articles in refereed journals

All Research Supervisors, academic staff and students are encouraged to conduct research and submit their work to peer-reviewed journals. Encouragement is by way of an honorarium for the successful submission of an article to a peer-reviewed journal and the mentoring of students and recent graduates by Research Fellows.

Completed research degrees

Over the years, AIB has gathered an impressive record of completed research degree theses. As the number of candidates is steadily rising, the number of completions will progressively increase too.

Work-applied MBA capstone projects

MBA students are required to complete a research project for their capstone subject using the case research method or reflective practice.

Work-applied collaborative research

New links are being negotiated with universities in Asia and elsewhere for collaborative research to be undertaken.

(b) Nexus between Research and Teaching

There is a nexus between research and teaching that is evident throughout the work of AIB. Work-Applied Learning has been the subject of ongoing research for many years, and the principles of this approach are incorporated across the curriculum. There are important linkages, as follows:

First, using their own research and practical experience, academics are able to facilitate effective learning, Some facilitators are themselves AIB research degree graduates and this process of returning knowledge is encouraged. Facilitators are not purely researchers but are also required to have practical managerial experience. Together, this provides a unique environment for learning.

Second, apart from their own research, facilitators invariably use materials produced by other researchers. Students are encouraged to read a selection of the latest articles in each subject, adding currency to student thinking and debate.

Next, students are constantly encouraged to do their own Work-Applied Research. One means is through the various course projects; another is through small research-type assignments, based on the idea of learning through discovery.

Further, the Gibaran Journal of Applied Management—using a 'double blind' review process—publishes some exceptional student work so that other students and a wider community of scholars and practitioners can learn from it.

Finally, staff and students are encouraged to investigate or undertake research that directly addresses education issues. For example, research about student learning styles has had an impact on the way we teach and the writing of study materials.

(c) Nexus between Research and Consultancy

As the corporate arm of AIB grows, it is clear that there is a close interrelationship with research activities. The nature of these links is as follows:

Firstly, a reputation for research in a particular area is regarded by clients as an important reason to engage AIB in consultancy. The point is made that AIB consultants are supported by up-to-date knowledge of their subject and are aware of the latest ideas.

Conversely, consultancy in 'live' projects adds to AIB's research base. Fresh information is collected and reports written as a part of such consultancies can result in related publications as case studies. Together, the links between research and consultancy strengthen the work-applied nature of AIB.

SPECIALISED QUALIFICATIONS IN WORK-APPLIED LEARNING

At AIB the development of managers in different aspects of Work-Applied Learning can be gained incrementally, with the option of proceeding progressively to higher levels of qualifications. It is up to the managers to decide how far to proceed along the path. Each of the qualification programs are designed such that managers can continue to work at the same time as they are attaining their qualifications. The various qualifications open to the managers are as follows:

a) Graduate Certificate in Work-Based Learning
b) Graduate Certificate in Action Learning
c) Graduate Certificate in Change Management
d) Master of Management (Work-Based Learning)
e) Master of Management (MMgt)
f) Doctor of Business Administration (DBA)
g) Doctor of Philosophy (PhD)

The research topics in the MMgt, DBA and Phd could be in Action Learning and WAL and Change Management.

SUMMARY

This chapter has shown how AIB has evolved from a work-based management consultancy to a global centre for Work-Applied Learning and research.

AIB continues to establish more Work-Applied Learning and research collaborations around the world.

REFERENCES

Australian Research Council 2008, <www.gove.au/default.htm>, viewed 16 May 2008.

Curtin University of Technology, Facilitating Excellence in Research Training, November 2007.

Hanson, D & Grimmer, M 2007, 'The mix of qualitative and quantitative research in major marketing journals, 1993-2002', European Journal of Marketing, vol. 41, no. 1-2, pp. 58-70.

Sobh, R & Perry, C 2006, 'Research design and data analysis in realism research', *European Journal of Marketing*, vol 40, issue 11/12, pp. 1194-1209.

Stokes, R & Perry, C 2007 'Chapter 10. Case research about enterprises' in Hine D and Carson D, (eds), *Innovative Methodologies in Enterprise Research*, Edward Elgar, Northampton, Massachusetts.

The Economist 2007, 'What is the point of research carried out in business schools?', 24Aug., available at <Economist.com>, viewed 16 May 2008.

Yin, R 1994, *Case Study Research: Design and Methods*, Sage, Newbury Park.

Zuber-Skerritt, O & Perry, C 2002, 'Action research within organisations and university thesis writing', *Organisational Learning*, vol. 9, no. 4, pp. 171-179.

ACKNOWLEDGEMENT

Acknowledgement is made to Emeritus Professor Chad Perry, whose work provides the basis for much of this chapter.

CHAPTER 7
REFLECTIONS

In the preceding chapters the reader will have joined me on a long journey. We started, in the first chapter, by reviewing the way that ideas about Work-Applied Learning using the fused ARAL approach have evolved. I explained how my own interest in this approach originated in the practical world of management development. From there, I saw the potential to create new opportunities for managers to learn and to apply it in their own workplace. They have also been able to gain educational recognition in the process. Indeed, it was through this transition that the present Australian Institute of Business was born.

Since then, learning and practice have gone hand in hand, the one informing the other in a recurring cycle. As a result, ideas have continued to evolve and the account given in this book represents what is, to me, the present state of play. To provide an early demonstration of their practical application, I have included a summary of two illustrative case studies. I hope that the reader will find Chapter 1 a useful starting point in this onward journey.

Theory and practice are inextricable, and so, having established a conceptual foundation, the next three chapters provide some 'real world' examples of Work-Applied Learning and change in practice. The case studies could not be more different, but that simply illustrates the very point in question, namely, that these concepts are applicable to a wide range of situations. They can be used to solve problems and introduce change in organisations, in one country or another.

Thus, in Chapter 2, we enter the arena of a government-based enterprise, Australia Post. In spite of the scale of this organisation and its complexity, it is required to perform a number of well-defined tasks, including, most obviously, the delivery of mail. To execute this efficiently, the system must be right and staff need to be properly trained and motivated. This represents quite a challenge, but one which is ideally suited to the application of Work-Applied Learning principles.

Teams were formed to review and improve processes and (as the chapter records) the outcomes were very positive.

In Chapter 3, the scene shifts to Malaysia and to a shipping conglomerate, the Global Carriers Group. In the throes of an economic crisis that was particularly severe in South-East Asia, the Group looked to Work-Applied Learning to reorientate itself. The approach enabled senior managers to work together to find the best ways not only to survive the crisis, but manage beyond that. Action Learning sets were formed and a new strategy was developed, based on consolidation rather than immediate growth. This enabled the corporation to weather the storm and emerge in a strong position for future growth. Participants in the program were all agreed that it was an effective process and that they had become better equipped to deal with change.

After Malaysia, Chapter 4 takes us to Papua New Guinea and, in this case, to a government department, the Internal Revenue Commission. The purpose of the WAL program here was to develop a strategic plan and to design a new structure for the organisation. This was a tough assignment, not least of all because there would be winners and losers in any restructuring, but the WAL approach proved to be well suited to the process. Importantly, it brings people together and the cyclical process allows time for reflection and continuing improvement. At the end of the process, individuals agreed that it had helped them to look beyond their immediate working situation, that their confidence had grown, and that they were better equipped to engage in decision making and leadership roles.

Following these three in-depth studies, the next chapter switches the spotlight to evaluation and validation. The purpose here is to show how a specific WAL program could subsequently be assessed, the case in question being a management development program for indigenous community leaders in South Australia. Following the implementation of the original program, the opportunity is taken to look back on the process and to identify key indicators of its effectiveness and reliability. The main stakeholders (not least of all, the community leaders themselves) were invited to participate in this latter process. Through a combination of qualitative and quantitative analysis, a positive response is recorded. Community leaders and other stakeholders were all agreed that the program had led to increased confidence and self-esteem, commitment, and the understanding and application of management skills and knowledge.

Against this background of theoretical and practical aspects of the WAL approach, Chapter 6 shows how AIB is becoming a global centre of WAL and research and why it is known as 'The Practical Business School'. Authority was obtained at an early stage to award postgraduate degrees through to doctoral level.

A cluster of research degree programs has provided a stimulus for associated research activity, based directly on student projects and also on the evolving interest of supervisors. For a small institution, AIB has achieved an enviable record of research degree completions and publications, around a shared theme of Action Research, Case Research and Reflective Practice.

So where does all this leave us now? Writing a book is like taking a photo of a landscape through the window of a moving train. No sooner is it recorded than the scene changes. Research is a journey without end, a sequence of connected snapshots.

WAL itself is an evolving concept. With the benefit of experience, it has changed in the past, and it will change further in the future. We are constantly learning and with each new study, there will be fresh issues to consider. In response to evolving experience, models of WAL will be constantly tested and refined. Moreover, the response to this book by managers and academics will also encourage further thought and the sharing of ideas. The spur to continuing progress will be welcome. Indeed, if this book serves only to lead to new developments in the field, it will have been more than worthwhile.

INDEX

Lightning Source UK Ltd.
Milton Keynes UK
UKOW05f2032040417
298345UK00017B/529/P